Post-Modernism on Trial

ALDO ROSSI, HOTEL IL PALAZZO, FUKUOKA, JAPAN

MICHAEL GRAVES, NEWARK MUSEUM, NEW JERSEY

Architectural Design
Edited by Andreas C Papadakis

Post-Modernism on Trial

KISHO KUROKAWA, SAITAMA PREFECTURAL MUSEUM OF MODERN ART, URAWA, SAITAMA

ACADEMY EDITIONS · LONDON

Acknowledgements:

This issue contains edited extracts from the following books:
Charles Jencks, *The Language of Post-Modern Architecture* , Academy Editions, London.
David Kolb, *Postmodern Sophistications*, University of Chicago Press, Chicago.
Philip Cooke, *Back To The Future*, Unwin Hyman Ltd., London.
The article by Vincent Scully *Animal Spirits* is reprinted from the October 1990 issue of *Progressive Architecture,* Copyright 1990, Penton Publishing.
Paul Goldberger *And Now, An Architectural Kingdom* first appeared in *The New York Times* in April 1990. Copyright ©1990 by the New York Times Company, Reprinted by permission.
The material on Hotel Il Palazzo was supplied by Minako Morita at Studio 80, Tokyo.
Photographs courtesy of the architects unless otherwise stated:
Front Cover by William Tayor; *pp 2, 24,* photographs by William Taylor; *pp 27, 30, 31, 32, 33, 35, 36-39* by Charles Jencks, *pp 45-55* photographs by Steven Brooke, *pp 56-65* photographs © ESTO Photographic/Peter Aaron; *pp 83-96* and Back Cover photographs by Nacása & Partners.

We would like to thank ESTO Photographics for their cooperation in the preparation of this issue.

EDITOR
Dr Andreas C Papadakis

EDITORIAL OFFICES: 42 LEINSTER GARDENS, LONDON W2 3AN TELEPHONE: 071-402 2141
CONSULTANTS: Catherine Cooke, Dennis Crompton, Terry Farrell, Kenneth Frampton, Charles Jencks, Heinrich Klotz, Leon Krier, Robert Maxwell, Demetri Porphyrios, Colin Rowe, Derek Walker.
HOUSE EDITOR: Maggie Toy ASSISTANT HOUSE EDITOR: Justin Ageros DESIGNED BY: Andrea Bettella, Mario Bettella
SUBSCRIPTIONS MANAGER: Mira Joka

First published in Great Britain in 1990 by *Architectural Design*
an imprint of the
ACADEMY GROUP LTD, 7 HOLLAND STREET, LONDON W8 4NA
ISBN: 1-85490-044-7 (UK)

The Publishers and Editor do not hold themselves responsible for the opinions expressed by the
writers of articles or letters in this magazine
Copyright of articles and illustrations may belong to individual writers or artists
Architectural Design Profile 87 is published as part of *Architectural Design* Vol 60 9-10/1990
Published in the United States of America by
ST MARTIN'S PRESS, 175 FIFTH AVENUE, NEW YORK 10010
ISBN: 0-312-06144-7 (USA)

Printed and bound in Singapore

HANS HOLLEIN, HAAS HOUSE, VIENNA

Contents

Architectural Design Profile No. 88
Post-Modernism on Trial

CHARLES JENCKS
DEATH FOR REBIRTH

In 1977, Architectural Design published extracts from the first edition of Charles Jencks' The Language of Post-Modern Architecture. Here, to coincide with the sixth, 1991, edition of the book, this new excerpt has been specially edited for Architectural Design. Jencks re-states his belief in pluralism, and assesses the Post-Modern movement in the wake of the controversy surrounding Prince Charles' Vision of Britain.

Now that Post-Modern architecture has triumphed around the world, many people have declared it dead. This, the fate of all successful movements, is something to be celebrated. Born in a fit of love, they grow to maturity all too quickly, are vulgarised, mass-produced and finally assigned to the scrap-heap of history. The same thing happened to Modernism so it is no surprise that those who arrived first at the morgue to certify the new Post-Modern corpse – and see it stayed buried – were none other than the Neo-Modernists. This occurred in 1982, and the participants at this convivial wake brought along doctored photographs of Michael Graves' Portland Building blowing up, as if to reassure themselves of the truth.

By 1986 – ironically, just when many of the world's largest architectural practices were shifting to a Post-Modern mode – the Italian magazine *Modo* announced with an air of revelation that the style was old hat. Not to be outdone at late discovery was the President of the Royal Institute of British Architects, who, in 1989, attacked the genre as 'bimbo architecture' and declared for the Year 2000: 'we simply cannot go to the Millenium Ball wearing the threadbare rags of Post-Modernism'. Out of fashion? If ever there were proof of a movement's continued vitality it was these obituaries and attacks, for who is going to waste time flogging a dead style? As if to underline this, the President promptly apologised for his flagellation of the anti-chic and asked a major Post-Modern architect for forgiveness. Such are the vicissitudes of the Style Wars.

Inevitably, the life and death of an architectural movement, like civilisation, is based on a biological metaphor: but, this is only somewhat relevant to anything as complex as an architectural language. Columns and curtain walls come and go irrespective of cultural health. However, many people felt liberated from the dogma and strictures of Modernism when, along with Peter Blake and other architectural medics, I took its failing pulse in the 1970s. As John Summerson later wrote of these diagnoses: 'in the 1980s it has become fashionable to declare the Modern Movement dead. As a serious statement this is arguable, but it is an interesting idea – perhaps the first really inspiring new idea since the Movement was born. It is, anyway, liberating'.

The notion of death frees one from the tyranny of the prevailing orthodoxy and since Modernism had a virtual stranglehold on the profession and academies from the late 1930s to the 1970s, many architects and much of the public were exhilarated. Modern architecture was no longer a necessity, and the idea of the *Zeitgeist* and technological determinism – or, indeed, any determinism – was discredited. Architecture could again be based on context, mood, culture, ornament, or almost whatever mattered to the architect and client. And, it has to be added today, the 'death of Post-Modernism' produced a similar relief, for that also loosened the bonds of professional doctrine and tyrannical fashion, and increased freedom of choice.

Pluralism versus Monism

Thankfully, today no single orthodoxy dominates Western society: neither the Pre-Modernism advocated by Prince Charles, the Neo-Modernism advocated by his adversary the President of the RIBA, nor the Post-Modernism caught in a cross-fire between the two camps. If anything reigns it is pluralism – and that 'ism' is incapable of ruling since it depends on fostering choice. There is a paradox here because pluralism is *the* Post-Modern ideology above all others. How can this condition exist without the triumph of the Post-Modern style? Because, as even the remaining Modernists now grant, we live in a post-modern era (lower case), the information age where plural cultures compete and there is simply no dominant cultural style or ethos. Or if, say, Deconstruction is fashionable in 1989, it is declared *passé* in two years – the average age of an architectural movement in the global village.

In the pre-industrial past, Traditional culture was the leading way of thought; during the industrial age Modernism became the most important *episteme;* while in the post-industrial period none of these competing cultures – High, Low, Traditonal, Mass, Pop, Ethnic or other – speaks for the majority of urban dwellers. Most of the time in the huge megalopolis we are all minorities – yes, even those who have cornered what used to be called 'the ruling taste', the Establishment. This can be alienating, and many people deplore the competition of language games and values, and the retreat into a previous othodoxy, whether Modern or Traditional. But those with a Post-Modern sensibility enjoy the diversity, and know why it is necessary and positive.

What is at stake in this situation, what constitutes the new world view? Fundamentally, it is the growing understanding that pluralism creates meaning; or put negatively in the cool terms of information theory, that 'where there is no difference, there is no information'. Variety of style and habitation generates meaning, because significance is generated by a field of tensions, or an oppositional system: a system concerned with much more than style. Any architecture signifies values and supports a way of life; and these are relational matters, as much as is any aesthetic.

Traditionalists and Modernists have one thing in common: they tend to dislike pluralism and suppress it. Consider Le Corbusier's injunctions: 'The "styles" are a lie . . . Our own epoch is determining, day by day, its own style' – that is, a single one based on industrialisation and the Machine Aesthetic. Or compare this monism with Prince Charles' norms of harmonisation. When he attacked the original scheme for extending London's National Gallery, he re-phrased the Modernist's plea for consistency: 'I would understand better this type of High-Tech approach if you demolished the whole of Trafalgar Square and started again with a single architect for the entire layout, but what is proposed is like a monstrous carbuncle on the face of a much loved and elegant friend.' The implication, with its heavy irony, is that a whole lot of aesthetically unified carbuncles would be acceptable.

The norm of stylistic harmony is upheld by architects the Prince favours – Quinlan Terry and Leon Krier – as much as it is by Late and Neo-Modernists. Lloyds' of London, the Hongkong Bank, the Arab Institute or little-red-fire-engine pavilions at the Parc de la Villette in Paris are all confined to a unity of material, time and mood – whatever their style. And this despite the fact that they are equivalent in size to a traditional village! When the classical unities become this dominant, when large chunks of the environment housing thousands of people are built at a stroke in the same manner, one can speak of a totalising impulse still prevalent with the Traditionalists and traditional Avant-Garde. *Plus ca change, plus c' est la même integration.*

The Post-Modern Paradigm

This is not true of Post-Modern urbanism. Large developments, such as the decade of building in Berlin under IBA, mix various architects, styles, ages and uses of buildings – sometime even on the same street. While common urban typologies such as the perimeter block are adopted, and some aesthetic rules of the game are imposed, various architects are also encouraged to produce difference, using oppositions within these frameworks. By the late 1970s, this became a norm which was demonstrated in the 1980 Venice Biennale: its *Strada Novissimma* was composed as a system of differences. Soon thereafter, Robert Krier and the Berlin planners under IBA adopted the policy of hiring multiple architects for a district, and combined this strategy with infill building and rehabilitation. By the mid 1980s, the policy had disseminated to developers – Broadgate in London, Battery Park City in New York, the Faneuil Hall complex in Boston and downtown Frankfurt were typical commercial versions of the idea. What had started in 1961, when the first shot of Post-Modernism was fired by Jane Jacobs in her book the *Death and Life of Great American Cities,* had now become a mini-orthodoxy. At least one quarter of all mega-developers saw the point of diversity: mixed ages, mixed uses and complexity made economic as well as aesthetic sense.

It's fascinating that the 'Jacobite manifesto' should fit in so well with the larger Post-Modern paradigm which was growing at the time, and that she should appreciate the fact: such self-awareness is rare. If one steps back from urbanism and architecture and looks at philosophy, literature and science, one finds the same general points emerging in the 60s: the interest in interconnection and symbiosis which characterise ecology; the preoccupation with diversity and difference which typify Post-Modern philosophy and politics; and the understanding of interrelated variables on which the new 'sciences of complexity' are built. At the end of her book, in a chapter called 'The Kind of Problem a City Is', Jacobs shows that urban questions are not particularly ones of 'simplicity', nor 'disorganised complexity' – both of which characterised Modern science from Newton to the development of statistics. Rather, a city is a *problem of organised complexity* like those with which the life sciences deal.

All the key Post-Modern sciences are rooted in this new *episteme* – ecology, ethology, biology, holography, the cognitive sciences, psycholinguistics, semiology, chaos theory, neural networks, and so on. Almost all of these deal with feedback, non-linear equations and sudden self-organising phenomena, whereas the Modern sciences, as Jacobs argues, deal with dual- or multi-variable statistical issues. The 'sciences of simplicity' – Newton's laws of gravity and the workings of the solar system are the prototypes – established the Modern paradigm, while the sciences of complexity – Noam Chomsky's ideas of deep structure, or Ilya Prigogine's of self-organisation are the archetypes – created the Post-Modern *episteme*. So we have an implicit consensus, or an overlap of thought patterns and heuristic models centring on pluralism and complexity. Organised complexity as idea, fact and style typifies the urbanism of Jane Jacobs, the architecture of

Robert Venturi and the literature of Umberto Eco – which is why these disparate manifestations help sum up the Post-Modern paradigm. Indeed, Venturi's *Complexity and Contradiction in Architecture,* 1966, is considered, after Jacobs' book, the second major treatise to start defining Post-Modern architecture.

What is Post-Modern Architecture?

Post-Modern architecture is obviously concerned with more than *pluralism* and *complexity*, although these two key words begin to locate its centre. To suggest the wealth of concepts involved in its definition, I will briefly summarise and emphasise some of the essential definers.

The primary strategy architects have created to articulate the pluralism of culture is that of *double-coding*: mixing their own professional tastes and technical skills with those of their ultimate clients – the inhabitants. Double-coding exists at many levels and has done so in several periods: it may be an ancient temple which mixes abstract geometry and representational sculpture, high and low art. It may be the Post-Modern Classicism of James Stirling that contrasts monumental and high-tech codes; or vernacular and commercial codes, as in the case of Charles Moore. The dualities invariably contrast the local with the contemporary – hence the label Post-*Modern*. But whatever the combination, it is the concept of coding itself which is essential to this growing tradition.

Modern architects simply perceived and constructed the meanings they cared about in architecture. By contrast, Post-Modernists are keenly aware that architecture is a *language* perceived through codes, and that codes and therefore actual seeing differs somewhat in every culture. Hence the complex relation of the architect to the client – again partly explicable by an emergent science of complexity, semiotics: the theory of signs. This theory is one of the crucial ways in which Post-Modern thought differs from its predecessor; but this article is about a growing tradition of architecture, not its intellectual foundations. I have tried to give just enough theory here to explain the main concepts of architectural semiotics and drive home the point that, for Post-Modernists, the perceptual codes of the users are just as important as those of the architects – another reason for double-coding. Modernists and Traditionalists, by contrast, focus on the producers.

There is more to Post-Modern architecture than its conception as a multi-level language. If one were to list the defining characteristics they would extend far beyond the four or five stylistic categories that historians usually apply to a period – for instance, the four that Hitchcock and Johnson found in the International Style in 1932. Anthony Blunt, in a polemical analysis, *Some Uses and Misuses of the Terms Baroque and Rococo as Applied to Architecture,* finds the historian cannot work with fewer than ten definers. It could be worse! In my own attempt to classify Late, Neo and Post-Modern architecture, I found at least 30 important design ideas, ideological definers and stylistic preoccupations – and there are obviously more. Architectural movements are as complex to define as bird species are for the taxonomist, and demand the synthesizing of many characteristics into a whole. The historian classifies overlapping sets of definers by family resemblances – as the philosopher Wittgenstein put it – and this is partly a global, and partly an inductive judgement.

The characteristics of the Post-Modern come from its attempt to cut across the spectrum of tastes with a variety of styles: thus it seeks a *radical eclecticism,* or a multiple-coding, as well as the double logic I have already mentioned. There are indeed more than 30 norms and forms which define the movement.

For other writers, the situation is somewhat simpler. In *The Doubles of Post-Modern,* 1980, the architect Robert Stern supports a 'traditional post-modernism' which is concerned with *historical continuity* and, like my own work, the 'struggle for cultural coherence that is not falsely monolithic': that is, one based on architectural 'form as communicating sign' which a wide public can understand. Elsewhere he mentions as essential an intense concern for *ornament, context,* and *historical allusion.*

Paolo Portoghesi, in *Postmodern, The Architecture of a Postindustrial Society,* 1982, not only places emphasis on the *information society,* but again on *historical continuity* and the role of *city typologies* in sustaining this. Thus Stern and Portoghesi, through their writing, architecture and exhibitions, have led the movement towards the historicism to which much of the public – sadly – reduces it. While their work often has a creative integrity, the genre which follows it is frequently commercialised rubbish.

The agenda is much larger and more important than the superficial facadism to which giant commercial commissions and the Disney Corporation have bent it. But there also *is* this weakness to a certain strain of the tradition. 'Disney World Postmodernism' and the kitsch versions of the genre, are the main reasons critics pronounce the movement dead while it still moves. It is true, however, that the other traditions show the same problems of overproduction; and these are *systemic.* The commercial and production viruses which contaminated Modern architecture are now attacking its child. 'Fast-Food-Mega-Build' – to give it as horrible a name as I can – corrupts all movements, and as long as architecture is produced on the run, in too great volume, it will suffer these problems of overproduction. They are, once again, diseases of success.

Heinrich Klotz, in *The History of Postmodern Architecture* (Germany 1984, USA 1988) offers a slightly different focus than that given here. He takes up the communicational aspect that all writers stress and bends it towards 'narrative content'. Form does not just follow function, in his definition of Post-Modern architecture, but 'fiction'. The concern for *Meaning in Architecture* (the subject of a book George Baird and I edited in 1969) becomes the central preoccupation for Klotz, and this very wide concern allows him to include many architects – Rem Koolhaas, John Hejduk and Richard Meier – who I (and no doubt they themselves) would be much happier to see in some other slot, perhaps marked 'Late-' or 'Neo-Modernist'. The three of them, like other New Moderns, have been attacking Post-Modernism since at least 1982.

Nonetheless, Heinrich Klotz is right to show the ambiguity of these practitioners – who all *revise, ironise,* and *distort* abstract Modernism – and in these weak senses are 'post'. But defining the movement by the single category 'fiction' or 'allusion and association', as he does elsewhere, is much too loose. All architecture has some representational and allusive meaning, even if it is to a previous abstraction or tradition of non-meaning (as in Hannes Meyer's work). So, otherwise exemplary as history, Klotz's definition of the subject is at once too wide in its inclusion of Neo-Modernists, and too narrow, in its reduction to 'fiction'.
All this dispute over categories and the intentions of a movement may sound academic, or irrelevant to architectural practice – but it is not. Differences of meaning create divergences in evolution – as we have seen in the Prince of Wales' recent battle, first with the Modernists, then with the Post-Modernists.

The Failure of Prince Charles' Crusade
In 1984, on the 150th anniversary of the RIBA, Prince Charles launched what he later termed a 'crusade' – against the heathens, nihilists, abstractionists and all those who were building an anti-Christian, materialistic architecture in Britain. Characteristically, in this Holy War, he copied the example of Post-Modernists and my own use of metaphors to attack the sterile malapropisms of Mies van der Rohe and those who prefer abstract sculpture to significance. Mies' proposed skyscraper for Central London he vilified and destroyed as a 'glass stump'. Other verbal missiles stopped the 'monstrous carbuncle' designed for the National Gallery, James Stirling's '1930s wireless' put forward also for

Central London, and the 'prison camp' proposed by Sir Philip Dowson and Arups for London's Paternoster site. As visual metaphors these exocets were wide of the mark, but as Royal bombs they were very effective. The Prince, surrounded by a coterie of Traditionalists and with TV and the newspapers egging him on, could not resist the temptation to sink the designs and reputations of England's finest professionals. He claimed in a *Sunday Times* article in 1989 that he did not have any real power, but the truth was that he did have great power to destroy.

The pity of all this is even greater. Prince Charles' misdirected crusade embodies a lot of common sense and has a following even among Modernists. Indeed, everybody who watches television knew by 1980 that tower blocks were out, that abstract Modernism was usually boring, and that rapacious development was the main cause of city deconstruction. James Stirling and Sandy Wilson – two of the Prince's victims – had been saying such things for 15 years; they were the clichés of the average professional. Furthermore, many architects were inclining towards pluralism and ready to accept the partial validity of his three Cs: Community Architecture, Classicism and Conservation. Ninety per cent of what Prince Charles advocates is beneficent, has been said before, and gains general assent; the problem is with the other ten per cent.

By attacking such humane and respected architects as Philip Dowson for being 'inhuman', by censoring his design for the St Paul's area as 'a prison camp' and calling it 'watered-down classicism' and 'half-hearted'; by intervening to influence developers and manipulate a democratic process, he has sent two very clear messages to the architectural profession: that he holds their values in contempt, and that he is prepared to act undemocratically.

The pity, again, is that he usually favours such things as participation in design and an open process of choosing architects. But encouraging developers from America, Japan and Britain to come, cap in hand, to his country estate Highgrove to present their schemes behind closed doors – and trim them to a Classicist cut – is no way for a Prince to behave. That's the style of the Old Boys' Network and the Watergate plumbers. And this from a Prince who has supported community architecture and minorities. Of monarchy he has even said, 'It can be an elective institution. After all, if people don't want it, they won't have it'.

This is rather how most architects felt by September 1989, the date of the Prince's one-sided book and television film *Vision of Britain,* with its accompanying exhibition at the Victoria and Albert Museum. Before this, many in the design community, including me, felt that the Royal intervention had at least publicity and populism to recommend it. While architecture was becoming ever more topical in other countries, the popular press in Britain had not really taken it up before 1984; so the Prince could gain a certain credibility over time simply by being the pretext for provoking public debate.

Vision of Britain changed all that. While a popular success in viewing and rating terms, it was not a hit with journalists, critics, architects or the Establishment. A characteristic opinion, by a respected historian and writer on country houses – Mark Girouard – spoke for the informed minority. The Prince's tastes were too predictably limited; like 'Pavlov's dog', Girouard wrote, 'when he sees a pitched roof, a chimney stack, a pediment, a column or a sash window, he wags his tail; when he sees concrete, or is deprived of his bowl of ornament, he barks'. This was devastating, coming from a writer both eminent in the field and one who shares much in terms of values and background with the Prince.

Such opinions were confirmed at the 'Official Debate' I had the misfortune to chair at the V & A near the close of the exhibition. It degenerated into name-calling, and showed very clearly the kind of climate which the Prince's attack had created in Britain. On my right, Lucinda Lambton and Leon Krier were pitted against Martin Pawley and Sandy Wilson sitting to the left. Once the debate started, I couldn't help remembering the origins of 'left- and right-wing' – categories architecturally determined by the seating positions of the two opposing camps in the Estates General at the time of the French Revolution.

I don't remember who threw the first parallel that night at the V & A. In any case, Prince Charles was compared to Pol Pot, then a Modernist to Honnecker, then the Prince of Wales to Stalin, then a Modernist to Ceaucescu, then the Prince to Hitler, then . . . In hindsight, I should have declared the meeting closed at that point, for the next two hours brought little light and much blood.

The only real conclusion was the vote at the end of the evening, which showed that the audience of over 300 generally approved of the Prince's intervention, but questioned his taste, and disliked his tactics. By an overwhelming majority they supported his focusing of public opinion on architecture; but by a vote of two to one they rejected his stylistic preferences, and by two and a half to one they disapproved of his methods of influencing planning decisions.

From his impregnable position of influence – with the BBC, *Sunday Times* and popular press giving him a virtual monopoly of the media-waves – he imposes his opinions and planning preferences and destroys reputations. The fact that, with many others, I agree with 90 per cent of what he says does not make up for the rest: neither the undemocratic tactics, nor the gratuitous slurs. The fact that with other critics, I may also indulge in Modernist-bashing, does not justify his insults either: whereas ours may wound, they may be answered in kind; but his have the power to kill (at least four London schemes so far). Such truths the professions have come to realise. Architects, planners, developers and journalists – precisely those whom the Prince should try to influence if he really cared about winning his crusade – are beginning to appreciate another underlying motive.

In a rare moment of self-disclosure the Prince once said that he envied the Pop musician Bob Geldof, and that he too wanted to lead a popular crusade – creating an equivalent of Geldof's world-wide concert to aid the starving. No doubt in supporting the Traditionalists, and, later, the ecological movement, the Prince has found two issues worth promoting. Furthermore, his creation of a summer school for training craftsmen and architects in the traditional virtues, and his commissioning Leon Krier and others to design part of a town in Dorchester are very positive moves of his crusade. But, because of the overkill and his vindictive attacks over a period of six years, he has polarised and frightened his dreaded enemy to the point where – irony upon irony – it has now become unified and gained a credibility and purpose it previously lacked. Neo-Modernism has been turned into a professional mainstream by these attacks. It is not only the Old Cold War that thrives on demonology.

The RIBA, with its Neo-Mod President leading ranks of Born-Again Modernists; youthful designers, whipped up into paroxysms of Royal-loathing by Martin Pawley crying 'Hitler, Pol Pot, Stalin'; and the average professional, confused in the crossfire – all reflect the impact of the Prince's crusade. Oh, melancholic and misdirected Prince, if you really want to change Britain then change the hearts and minds of those who lead it: insults merely entrench and enhance your enemy.

Trumpet

What has all this tempest in a Royal-Isle to do with Post-Modernism? First of all, it has taken media attention away from this tradition, which is a good thing, just at the point in the 1980s when it was becoming a major approach for most firms around the world. That decade, in retrospect, shows the simultaneous growth of at least three separate movements: Traditional, Modern and Post-Modern. The building boom in the West and the growth of pluralism have meant that, paradoxically, all sides have been winning the Style Wars. Usually in architectural history, different approaches wax and wane in opposition. But every now and then, when the economic and cultural conditions are right, there is a sudden, mutual flowering of different traditions, just as in evolutionary history there can be a simultaneous explosion of new species – all prospering for a time. This can be conceived, visually, as the expanding end of a trumpet.

We are entering a new period of world communications where literally hundreds of styles and ways of life will thrive simultaneously cheek-by-jowl. They may not appreciate or understand each other. But tolerance, a respect for difference, an enjoyment of variety are *the* attitudes suited to the information age, and pluralism is its philosophy. Post-Modern writers such as David Lodge have insisted on the truths of dialogue and 'dialogic'; urbanists such as Jane Jacobs have shown the economic and social benefits which flow from a varied city fabric; and semioticians such as Umberto Eco have shown how a plural field of discourse creates the precondition for meaning. Such philosophies, major ideas and practices are now in the air, if not dominant. We are well into the post-modern era whether or not the Post-Modern Movement enjoys widespread favour in any particular place.

My own preference is that it remain one voice among many – that it not dominate a city or culture. When it does, at Disney World, the results are, to say the least, unfortunate and, hard to believe, even Modernist. True Post-Modernists really do believe in a field of tensions, in the necessity for Traditional and Modern approaches to flourish, in order to sustain all of their meanings. And so, opposed to the reigning ideologies of Prince Charles and the President of the RIBA, they do not want a crusade, or victory over the enemy. They realise the enemy is themselves in another mood and cultural situation, and that the system of oppositions must be supported as an end in itself. No difference? – no richness, no meaning.

DAVID HARVEY
LOOKING BACKWARDS ON POSTMODERNISM

'We feel that postmodernism is over,' a major United States developer told Moshe Safdie in 1988, adding that 'for projects which are going to be ready in five years, we are now considering new architectural appointments.' By 1990 we find a headline in the New York Times Arts section reading that 'As death comes to everything, so it comes to postmodernism.' While such announcements of its

'death' may be premature, the postmodern 'movement' (if it deserves such an appellation) definitely appears rather jaded. It looks more and more like an epiphenomenon of the 1980s (a product of the profligate, credit-fuelled entrepreneurialism of the Reagan-Thatcher years?) rather than the opening to some brave new world of the 21st century. Too many people have vested interests in it, of course, for it to succumb without a fight and that is quite properly so, for while its detractors might wish it would sink without a trace, there has been, quite simply, far too much going on under the heading of the postmodern that is worth saving for it to be arbitrarily dismissed. Periodic explorations of the sort that postmodernism attempted become eminently worthwhile if we are prepared to learn and act upon their lessons.

Evaluation is hard because, as everyone freely admits, postmodernism is difficult to pin down. Was it a style? Or a historical movement that had a definite purchase upon our imaginations for only a certain time, and only in a certain place? The most obvious answer is that it was probably both: a period in the advanced capitalist countries which began sometime between the mid-60s and mid-70s and began to fade in the 1990s, during which certain elements of style, for which many precursors and historical precedents could be found, became hegemonic. So what were the elements of style? Here the answers vary according to discipline and metier – postmodern music, dance, architecture, novels, theology, philosophy, sociology, geography, anthropology all had their distinctive variants as to what the rules of postmodern engagement might be, even though there was plenty of cross-fertilisation of ideas from one to the other.

The commonalities which I emphasised in *The Condition of Postmodernity* were a rejection of any overarching propositions (theories or meta-narratives or universalist styles), acceptance of pluralism and fragmentation (of language games or interests or interpretive communities), emphasis on difference (or otherness) and heterogeneity, and, finally, a wan or ironic admission of the ephemerality of things. As such, postmodernism defines a certain *positionality* (rather than the death) of the subject towards knowledge creation, cultural production, politics and the changing historical geography of daily life. And it was this positionality, I would argue, that provided the common link between the various currents of postmodernism, however diverse the actual outcomes were between the different disciplines and metiers. How deep this postmodern worm burrowed into our subconscious and how lasting the effects might be is hard to tell. To begin with, much that has happened over the past 20 years was neither post nor even particularly anti-modern. And here Charles Jencks' distinction between postmodern and late modern is instructive.

Post-Modernism is fundamentally the eclectic mixture of any tradition with that of the immediate past. It is both the continuation of Modernism and its transcendence. Its best

works are characteristically double-coded and ironic, making a feature of the wide choice, conflict and discontinuity of traditions, because this heterogeneity most clearly captures our pluralism.

Late modernism, on the other hand,

is pragmatic and technocratic in its social ideology and from about 1960 takes many of the stylistic ideas and values of Modernism to an extreme in order to resuscitate a dull (or clichéd) language.

As Jencks freely admits, it is not always easy to distinguish one style from the other since individuals frequently merged their concerns and produced all sorts of hybrids. And examples of the 'purest' (if that is even a reasonable term to use in this instance) form of postmodernism are rare enough to make them seem the product of the avant-garde fringe, rather than the hegemonic mainstream which many now are reconstructing in their instant histories of artistic and intellectual currents in the 1980s.

Yet, I would argue, both late and postmodernism share a basic positionality of the creative subject (they just differ in the nature of the project) and it is from this standpoint that I would want to write the turbulent history of intellectual and cultural perspectives over the last 20 years. The key question, then, is why was it that a particular positionality appeared as the only logical or reasonable one to take no matter whether one was working in architecture, philosophy, anthropology or literary theory. There are three levels of explanation to which we can appeal.

First the adoption of a new position from which to argue, sketch, depict or draw the world, can be interpreted in terms of the *exhaustion* of, or *reaction against* the old. There is always an element of truth in such an argument, an element that becomes a vast and overwhelming story of personal antagonisms and rivalries (sometimes between generations) in all of those inward-looking and myopic histories of disciplines and cultural forms. Is it not passing strange, though, that the sense of exhaustion or of some powerful urge to react against established orthodoxies should simultaneously occur in so many disciplines, and take the broadly parallel forms that they did? And do not stories of this sort inevitably imply, as the New York Times headline suggests, that once postmodernism became orthodoxy and authority it, too, must necessarily exhaust itself or be reacted against?

This brings us to the second line of argument which attributes an across-the-board movement like modernism or postmodernism to some changing and sometimes hidden zeitgeist in the world of thought and creative endeavour. Cultural and intellectual historians have certainly highlighted, both to their delight and ours, hidden connections between seemingly disparate currents of activities. Carl Schorske's *Fin de Siecle Vienna* is just one such work that pioneered the way in innumerable enquiries into the hidden connections that somehow seemed to link art, science, architecture, psychoanalysis and literature in that one place, during a certain historical period. Charles Jencks' enquiries into postmodern architecture are very much in this genre, illustrating how postmodern architecture took up and expressed themes that could be found in innumerable other corners of cultural and intellectual activity.

Enlightening and unfailingly interesting though such accounts may be, they always seem to lack something. At their best, they often allude to what it is they lack: some grasp of that common grounding of experience which leads people, without conscious aforethought, to explore certain creative paths rather than others.

Where, then, do such zeitgeist shifts come form? Are they pure manifestations of spirit, as Hegelians might maintain, or can we pin them down to the shifting world of that material experience which is the field for intellectual and creative action? If the latter, then how can we best depict that world? Here, of course, innumerable candidates present themselves. For example, the changing patterns of urban life in the 19th and 20th centuries have been closely looked at, with a good deal of credibility, in relation to the histories of modernism and postmodernism. And then there always lurks in the background that vulgar Marxist interpretation of 'base and superstructure' in which superstructural forms like art and architecture are regarded as some epiphenomenon of those Satanic underlying forces of the economy which, 'in the last instance' are always determinate.

It is, of course, the primary thesis of *The Condition of Postmodernity* that it is possible to pin the origins of postmodernism down and to explain why it was that so many people, in so many walks of life found it so impelling to adopt the particular positionality they did. I there suggested that the first major crisis of post-war capitalism in 1973-5 led to a series of political and economic adjustments which changed the field of experience for all of us in the advanced capitalist countries in profound ways. The post-war world had been constructed under U.S. military and economic hegemony, with the clear division set up by the Cold War; a power system based on the nation state and a production-political system that might broadly be described as Fordist (mass production and mass consumption) and Keynsian (state interventionist and based upon a political balance between labour, capital and other political forces within the nation state). We might not have fared well and there were discontents a-plenty, but this was a reasonably secure world in the sense that a dominant authority flourished and it was relatively easy to understand the contours of conflict and the dominant rules of the game. It was possible to assume the positionality as artist or intellectual of either for or against a fairly stable configuration of political power and cultural authority. Those against produced the free-speech movement in Berkeley, the inner city insurrections and civil rights movements in the United States, Woodstock, Andy Warhol, the '68 movements in Paris, Mexico City and Prague, and the like.

The certainties and stability dissolved all too rapidly, however, under the pressure of the economic collapse of the early 1970s and the subsequent recession of 1979-81. The collapse of the Berlin Wall and the end of the Cold War is one of the final elements of collapse of the verities of the post-war world. The experience of fresh fragmentations in the labour process (the changing division of labour), geographical shifts in the spaces of production (the competitive shift to Japan and the newly indus-trialising countries), volatility in the value of money (inflation-ary surges and exchange rate shifts) and an accelerating competitive concern to explore heterogeneity — both politically (the new social movements of ecology, anti-racism, feminism, cultural

decolonisation) and in terms of consumption (the search for secure consumer niches in a much more competitive world) — altered our positionality in relation to the production and secur-ing of access to material wealth. It is here tempting, of course, to invoke the base-superstructure thesis and simply interpret postmodernism as the outcome in the world of thought and creative action of these deeper economic transitions.

But I think a subtler interpretation is in order. To begin with, the world of cultural and intellectual production has become so caught up in the circulation of capital (the art market, the book trade, the music industry) that it scarcely makes sense now, if it ever did, to think of activities of this sort as reflections of, rather than as being directly implicated in the direct and competitive seeking of profit. Architects are beholden to developers; it is, in the end, the latter who call the tune and it is foolish to presume anything otherwise. Yet if, as Marx had it, what distinguishes the worst architects from the best of bees is that the former erects a structure in imagination first, then the harnessing of imaginative powers has always been central to the speculative development of capitalism as a social system. The buying and selling of imaginative capacity is one of the primary transactions in any capitalist economy. The base-superstructure model does not hold.

So where, then, does postmodernism come in? The thesis I considered in *The Condition of Postmodernity* rested primarily on an exploration of the changing experience of space and time, particularly in the period after the collapse of 1973. I attach particular importance to this, because the definition of space and time is essential to the creation of any sense of individual or collective identity — we define who we are, in large degree, through locating ourselves against the background of secure space-time co-ordinates. But when those co-ordinates shift, become insecure, it is very hard to know who we are. What time are we in — the 24 hours of the City broker, the 100 year or so history of most nation states, or the long-term time of global warming? What space do we inhabit — the village, the nation, Europe, the West, the globe? The subject did not 'die' as many suggested, but it certainly lost its bearings. The search was on to reconstruct identity precisely because our positionality with respect to the world had been changed, not because we were bored with the old (though the events of '68 suggested there was plenty of that around), but because the time and space of world affairs had shifted. The world of futures markets and global trading, coupled with changing access to the world's goods (ethnic foods and restaurants) and spaces (the advent of mass-tourism, instant communication across the airwaves and the like), rapid shifts in lifestyles and fashions, all created an atmosphere of uncertainty, volatility, and deep personal insecu-rity on even such fundamental matters as jobs, the values of money, and relations (across space and time) with others.

I call this kind of intensity of experience 'space-time compres-sion.' It has happened before in the history of capitalism (the coming of the railroads and the telegraph and a mass daily press did it in the mid 19th century, as did the advent of radio, the completion of the rail network and the vast wave of corporate mergers and cartel formation, and the carving out of world trading empires in the difficult period before the First World War). The effect, quite simply, is to put identity up for grabs. Our positionality necessarily changes because the space-time co-ordinates of social life have become like shifting sand rather than set securely in concrete.

Postmodernism was, I would suggest, a wide-ranging set of arguments constructed in and around this background of time-space compression. The diversity of both its offerings and its critical reception have to be understood in terms of the search for identity in a world of changing space-time horizons. It had its liberatory and celebratory side, of course. Those bored with the old could, as it were, reconstruct themselves in a new image precisely because new openings were created. The flourishing of creative endeavours, all the way from a revolutionary entrepreneurialism in the economy to similar impulses in the arts was certainly exciting for those that made it. And the serious exploration of the meaning of community, place, politics and ecology in a world in which time and space horizons were undergoing a radical restructuring provided for much that is positive in human endeavour.

Yet the down-side of postmodernism was also very strong. Its narrow engagement with entrepreneurialism and money values, its grasping of the nettle of ephemerality as if cultural production was but a branch of the futures market, its ransacking of history and places for ideas and images as if history and geography constituted nothing more than a vast supermarket of metaphors rather than a real history of struggle, of lives lost and lived out, often under conditions of the grossest oppression and repression of the human spirit. At its worst, it sought to construct an artificial and ersatz sense of time and space to replace the secure sense that had been lost. It dallied with the heritage culture, it pandered to nostalgia for a lost past, it pursued a narrow and parochialist cultural politics of place, and it shamelessly sold itself to the highest bidder without a shred of critical resistance. Above all, and this is Jencks' critical mistake, it mistook eclecticism for careful and respectful negotiation of cultural, political and social difference.

Why, then, is all of this in turn collapsing, and into what are we moving? Could it be that we are gradually adjusting to this new sense of time and space, coming to terms with the shifting co-ordinates that define identity and so finding it more and more possible to define a more secure positionality from which to argue or create? And could it be, also, that through the whirlwinds of political, economic and cultural change that have swept around us, we can still discern some very old problems; the extraordinary concentrations of economic and political power (whether in the financial system or the global media), the reterritorialisation of the globe into potentially antagonistic trading empires (North America, Europe, Japan), all in a context of mass powerlessness, of environmental degradation.

What postmodernism taught us was that difference and hetero-geneity matter, and that the language in which we represent the world, the manner of discourse, ought to be the subject of careful reflection. But it did not teach us how to negotiate differences in fruitful ways, nor did it tell us how to go about the business of communicating with each other after we had carefully deconstructed each others' language. And it is from this standpoint that the prefix 'post' is at least quite apt, for it avoids engagement with the question of what it is that we might be 'pre'. The return to realism, the movement away from the realm of metaphor and semiotics, and re-engagement with the realms of real politics and economy is, from this standpoint, to be welcomed. Looking backwards, postmodernism has much to teach as well as to lament. As we turn more carefully to the examination of the future, it is important that we do so in ways that reflect those lessons well.

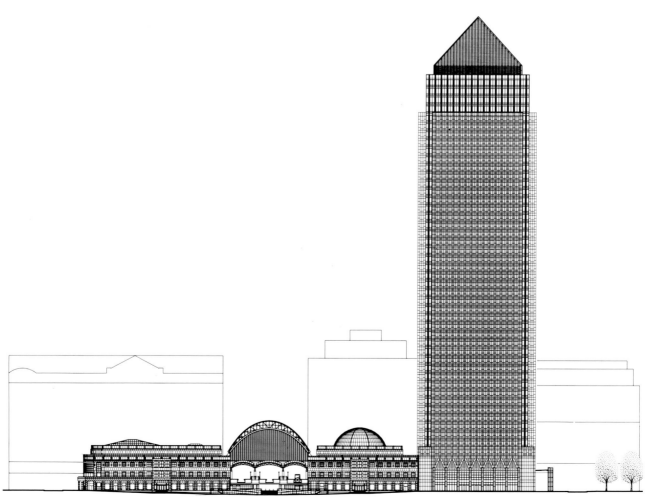

CESAR PELLI, CANARY WHARF, LONDON

DAVID KOLB
POSTMODERN SOPHISTICATIONS

The great modern architects thought we were growing into a unified technological world that would express itself in an architecture that was direct and honest with its forms. Most postmodern architects claim the dramatic simple forms of modern architecture are passé, and we cannot recapture the straightforward spirit in which they were built. We postmoderns see how codes and cultures multiply and

transgress, and we are not at home in any of them. When we build we must express the spirit of our age by manifesting the limits of any vocabulary through an ironic twist or mixture of different idioms.

The phrase *postmodern architecture* now has too many uses, but it still has some value. In general, it connotes the end of the modern ideal of pure form, and the removal of the modernist barriers to historical reference. In the popular press, the word seems most often applied to designer tall buildings that have historical ornament and some gestures towards the local context. For smaller buildings, the word often connotes a certain vocabulary of arches, curved windows, smooth but blocky shapes with historical appliqué, and the like.

There is a postmodern ironic historicism in the buildings of Charles Moore, Robert Stern and Ricardo Bofill. There is a deconstructive architecture in recent projects of Peter Eisenman and Bernard Tschumi. There is the postmodernism of images and simulacra; a shopping mall might capture this, though the most appropriate architecture for this vision of our world would be a cube whose surfaces, inside and out, provided screens for projections that would change the building into any and every style.

Charles Jencks, who helped popularise the term postmodern in architecture, urged applying it to buildings, such as many designed by Charles Moore, that use historical forms and ornament without belonging to any one definite historical style, and that have a self-consciously ironic or playful tone. Jencks calls this double-coding, where a building speaks in a local vernacular but also makes ironic commentary upon its own language. In more recent writings Jencks, seeks to appropriate the term especially for buildings that rework the classical and neo-classical vocabularies. Jencks' proposed meanings for the term apply to those buildings that have received the most press, such as Moore's Piazza d'Italia, Michael Graves's Portland and Humana buildings, and recent works by James Stirling.

A somewhat wider meaning was given the term by Paolo Portoghesi, who defines as postmodern any building that breaks the modern prohibition against historical reference, whether with ironic self-commentary or with vernacular earnestness. A still wider sense would include all of the above as well as buildings that break other modern prohibitions. A building with applied decoration that was neither ironic nor historical would still be postmodern by this wide criterion.

If we wished to include deconstructive architecture under the label *postmodern*, we would have to extend that term even further. All the senses thus far considered involve some movement away from abstraction and towards representation. Deconstructive architecture contests both sides of that duality. Thus I suggest that we distinguish between postmodern and deconstructive architecture, even though in philosophy and criticism the label *postmodern* is used by proponents of deconstruction to describe their own thought.

Most of what I say is aimed at the 'standard' postmodernism described by Jencks and Portoghesi. My concern is with the re-entry of history into architecture, whether this is in a revivalist or ironic manner. I am not claiming that this is the important feature of current architecture, but whatever the fate of the current styles that receive the label postmodern, the modernist prejudice against history will is no longer dominate design. I will be questioning theories that view our relation to history as either simple inhabituation or as detached criticism and ironic manipulation.

The Postmodern World

If the cosmic pillar of early shrines speaks of the centred fixity attributed to traditional society, modernity finds its emblem in the functional pilotis of Le Corbusier, and postmodernity in the oversized columns of Bofill and the invisible hitching posts in the parking lots of Las Vegas.

While in architecture the term *postmodern* has had its vogue and is beginning to fracture, in philosophy the phrase *postmodern thought* has been increasingly used to describe movements influenced by Nietzsche and Heidegger. Among the movements loosely labelled postmodern, deconstructive thought is the closest to Heidegger. It refuses to proclaim a postmodern era, for that would be to fall into the modern pattern of seeking continual novelty. Rather, we come to experience the limits and the self-undermining of modernity, without being able to escape into a new age.

Going on from what Heidegger says concerning the finitude of any revelation of the being of things, deconstruction sees a permanent tension between the modern claim to unity and its own self-limitation within a dispersion that escapes such unification, while making it possible. Showing this tension and self-transgression within the very texts and claims of the tradition, deconstructive thought helps undermine modern claims to control, order, and transparent rationality. But it does not replace them. Rather, it attempts to locate them within a space that they do not dominate. This has the effect of critique, though not one that proceeds from rival first principles.

Deconstruction concerns our manner of dwelling and does not itself provide any substantial meaning for a new home. There is no home in which we can dwell as we desire. Instead of inventing new styles, we manoeuvre the pieces of the old to express and undermine their unities. In architecture this can lead to the deliberately frustrated centrings and self-references in Peter Eisenman's House X, or to the divergences from unified form and the traditional goals of building in the projects of Bernard Tschumi. I will argue later that such works have a crucial though marginal role to play in the postmodern City.

The most self-proclaimed postmodern thought is identified with Lyotard, who at times speaks confidently of a new age (although he is more circumspect than many of his followers). As we saw in an earlier chapter, for Lyotard our age is losing the total meanings characteristic of both tradition and modernity. The central self is a myth, and its pure rationality gives way to a diversity of language games and practices that are irreducible to each other. Amid this plurality we should play our games lightly and ironically, inventing new rules as we go. No one game can define us and there is no pure meta-game above them all. Innovation is possible, and we need, for our liberation, constantly to invent new moves, new language games, new ways of being. We are caught within the infinite displacement of images (or of signifiers, simulacra, surfaces, intensities, and so on) and we should swim buoyantly in that flow rather than seeking firm ground.

Lyotard's postmodernity is an explicit extension of the avant-garde modernism that insisted on continual novelty, at the expense of the modernism that urged rationality and control. This is the reverse of the modern architect's preference for rationality over avant-garde experimentation. For Lyotard the rational society is the terror we must battle. In its concrete form that terror is the impersonal flow of international capital and its technology of control. Lyotard does not see this in orthodox Marxist terms, which still accept one grand story that aligns all history. Lyotard does not reject technology, which he sees as potentially liberating. Computer technology played a central role in the exhibition of our postmodern sensibility that Lyotard organised in Paris. Lyotard's vision of a fragmented yet technologically connected postmodern world resembles that of Jean Baudrillard, who is hardly so optimistic about our chances for creative innovation, because for him the play of simulacra washes out the differences (between language games) that Lyotard wants to promote.

To express and support this new age postmodern architecture needs a proliferation of styles, and new games played with the old pieces. While Lyotard's thought can be taken as calling for more novelty than deconstructive thought, both have been used to justify an architecture that uses historical reference ironically. For the most part, however, postmodern ironic historicism does not need Lyotard and Heidegger; its theories speak the language of semiotics and structuralism.

Hegel's description of the painter who has no substantive identity with the content of his art seems appropriate for these architects. Now the question returns: if there is no deep dwelling to be rediscovered and integrated into our building, if we are to be deconstructive or to invent new moves and games, if, in Hegel's terms, there is no substance of our consciousness, then have we escaped the distanced modern selfhood described by Weber and Hegel? Or is postmodernism just modern subjectivism with a stylish costume?

Irony and the Suspended Architect
We might have expected that when the modern prohibition against historical references weakened, architects would relax into older traditions, or begin new ones, and get on with building readable structures that fit our world. Vernacular and 'invisible' architecture could be approved again. Give architecture back to the people!

Such slogans have been heard, but they have not set the trend. We see distanced subjects playing with history, double-coding, irony, applied decoration, complexity and contradiction. This is different from modernist planners banishing history, but the distance remains. Why don't we find architects being praised in the media for devoting themselves to non-ironic development of traditional motifs?

> While postmodernists acknowledge history, many seem compelled to torture it until an 'original' contribution to artistic Progress has been made . . . A tangible burden of guilt still weighs on those who would deal with the past un-self-consciously, without coyness or irony. To regain fluency in the traditional language of design – and to make the product

of such a collaboration with past centuries accessible to a broad cross section of society . . . requires a redefinition of the very heart of artistic creativity. (Brolin,1985)

What are we to make of this? Is it just a passing condition soon to change once a residual modernist sensibility wears off? Or is it a matter of media bias and marketing strategies, to last as long as ironic buildings can charge higher rents? Or is it because the architects are trained to play elitist games and can't settle down with the people? Or are the architects victims of bad philosophy turned into dogma? Or is it perhaps because our world itself is multiply coded, ironic, complex and contradictory? It is the last alternative that links architectural practice to postmodern philosophy and criticism. I partly agree with this diagnosis, though later I stress the difference between claiming that we must express the unified spirit of our plural age, and claiming that there is no unified spirit of our age that we must express. For now, we need to look at the self-consciousness implicit in the ironic imperative.

Buildings that play ironic games lead a risky life. Suppose that a building has been carefully designed with ironic references to past styles. As time goes on and the building is used, do the ironic references and undertones survive? Or are they smoothed out as the building takes on its own immediate identity?

Still, it can be argued that if postmodern irony is not always perceived by the average user, it continues to be evident to the informed professional. Jencks canonised this division with his notion of 'double-coding'.

> One must start by defining a basic opposition in coding between the inhabitant and the professional, perhaps taking as one departure point Basil Bernstein's fundamental distinction between 'restricted' and 'elaborated' codes . . . a popular, traditional one which like spoken language is slow-changing, full of clichés and rooted in family life, and secondly a modern one full of neologisms and responding to quick changes in technology, art and fashion as well as the avant-garde of architecture.

Notice that Jencks has here almost reproduced the division between traditional and modern consciousness that furnished the basis for the story of modernity told by Weber and others. Jencks differs from the modern story in that he allows the postmodern artist no pure language or formally neutral point of view. But the fast-moving, professional code holds a position above local tradition just as the modern architect's rationality placed him above history.

The concepts Jencks uses in his argument for 'double-coding' are basically modern. This can be seen in his argument on why we cannot ever return to a single level of coding.

> There is an unbridgeable gap between the elite and popular codes, the professional and traditional values, the modern and vernacular language, and since there is no way to abolish this gap without a drastic curtailment in possibilities, a totalitarian manoeuvre, it seems desirable that architects recognise the schizophrenia and code their buildings on two levels.

A return to one-level coding, such as was urged by Brolin in the quotation above, is impossible because 'double-coding' allows more *possibilities*. This argument resembles Weber's: the special professional self-consciousness keeps us apart from premodern methods of building and increases our freedom.

Some who talk about postmodern architecture speak as if with the modernist barriers down we can roam freely through the past, taking historical allusions and forms from where we will for our 'double-coding' or ironic enjoyment. The fall of the modernist prohibition against historical reference coincides with a new world where history is available but we are not restricted by the premodern traditions. We, in our self-consciousness, can use all of history as our material.

> Architecture can now recycle in new syntactic contexts traditional forms, taken from anywhere. The world now emerging is searching freely in memory, because it knows how to find its own 'difference' in the removed repetition and utilization of the entire past . . . History is the 'material' of logical and constructive operations, whose only purpose is that of joining the real and the imaginary through communication mechanisms whose effectiveness can be verified. (Portoghesi, 1983)
> Why, if one can afford to live in different ages and cultures, restrict oneself to the present, the locale? Eclecticism is the natural evolution of a culture with choice. (Jencks, 1977)

We recognise here the Nietzschean will to power that appropriates the already formed and revalues it into a new meaning. This attitude gets results: Venturi puts a temple in the garden; Isozaki puts the Campidoglio at Tsukuba; Krier wants to put a ziggurat at La Villette. The architects seem to roam freely. And they are creatively changing their historical originals for the new context: the temple is a decorated shed; the Japanese Campidoglio conspicuously lacks a heroic central focus; the ziggurat would be a hotel.

We are told that we can do this because we hold historical content within a new self-consciousness. Unlike our literal minded ancestors and eclectic 19th-century grandparents (not to mention our narrow modern parents), we understand the nature of coding and the semiotics of architecture and, in that awareness, can use all of history as material for play. Our eclecticism is different; in Jencks's terms it is 'radical' rather than 'weak' because we can choose styles based on a developed semiotic theory.

All this sounds suspiciously like Gropius, who believed that the modern style was not a style at all but a free creation based on logic and technology, which one arrived at by abandoning styles and following the strict logic of function. For the postmodern theorists quoted above, history provides a space for free movement. Of course they are not saying that we should follow a strict logic of function. What they are saying is that the postmodern architect stands toward history differently because of a special self-consciousness. But that is what the modern movement claimed. Moderns and postmoderns disagree about historical reference, but is that significant? No style, all styles, what's the difference?

Polemics against modern architecture attacked as naive the modern belief that its forms would fit the new industrial world everywhere. This missionary and colonising attitude is said to have reduced architecture to a few mute words about power and efficiency. Postmodern architecture is supposed to respect local semiotic codes and taste cultures. Architects and theorists speak of the need to adopt (and adapt) the language of the community and its unavoidable cultural archetypes. The free play of imagination is to be tempered by the need to communicate, to make a legible architecture that fits its context, to be, in Venturi's words, 'expert in current conventions.'

This seems to leave the architect curiously suspended, dipping into 'their' context for a particular commission. Once the architect understands the client's vocabulary and codes, the building can use conventional elements for legibility, with 'high art' supplying the twists and ironies that delight other architects.

This chameleon facility with local codes, this ability to understand the native tribe and its language while remaining above it all, doesn't it sound suspiciously like Weber's social scientist, who dwells nowhere, even in his modern home?

The modern architect disdained historical codes, believing our civilisation had advanced to a universal pure language of form. The postmodern architect sees through all historical codes, believing our civilisation has advanced to a vision of ironic plurality. Is the postmodern architect just another distant modern self who happens to have other goals for the exercise of instrumental rationality?

If we would escape the modern, we must avoid the temptation of saying that after the complete barrier between the architect and history we now have a complete freedom with history. To flip from no access to total access is to stay within the modern. Perhaps we need to envision more carefully what would be truly beyond the modern: the switch from 'all or none' to 'some.'

The really non-modern idea would be that the architect's inhabitation of the world does not involve the modern ideal of total freedom and flexibility, even in its postmodern guises. We have to understand differential availability. Not every local code can be entered into. We are not modern detached subjects, and yet we do live in a self-consciously multiple world.

If we try to think through just how the architect's own activity is located and finite, we may find that we can have styles and contents of our own, yet with awareness and practices that do not reduce either to traditional fixity or to modern distance. We may find our historical dwelling, one that is not unified, but one for which we care in a way that is neither rational administration nor ironic play.

Haughty and Humble Ironies

Irony has become a buzzword in postmodern circles; nowadays even buildings are ironic. Whom can you trust?

The word irony comes from the Greek noun *eiron*, which describes a sly dissembler, a person with a smooth way of taking people in by hiding his strengths. Aristotle speaks of a quality he calls *eironeia* that consists of understating one's own good qualities. He considers this the vice at the other extreme from boastfulness. The virtue of straightforwardness stands between these two. Irony in Aristotle has more to do with a trait of character than with a literary turn. Maybe in the end it still does.

Classical rhetoric defines irony as calling something by an opposed name, for instance blaming someone through praising them, as Socrates praises his opponent while deprecating himself. After a long history in commentaries and books on rhetoric, during which the word was used to discuss a wide variety of attitudes and tropes, irony moved into discussions of art, especially in the 19th-century with the Schlegels, Solger, Kierkegaard and others. Most recently Charles Jencks has called 'ironies or complexities of reference . . . the defining characteristic of postmodernism.'

My concern here is to understand some varieties of postmodern irony. Much of what goes under the name postmodern irony still presupposes something like the superior distanced selfhood typical of modernity, though some deconstructive irony escapes this connection. However, the irony we find so far in postmodern architecture is not as subtle as the irony in postmodern literature and critical theory.

I will start by discussing the everyday notion of irony and some conditions for the success of irony as a speech act. Features of the everyday notion extend quite far into the refined philosophical and artistic meanings. I will be following two such features: the need of a firm platform from which to be ironic, and an act of superior judgment. Later in, the discussion we will come to types of irony that question these features.

One popular dictionary describes irony as occurring when the literal meaning of a statement is the opposite of the intended meaning, especially when this understates the intended meaning. The dictionary goes on to speak of irony as, 'especially in contemporary writing, a manner of organising a work so as to give full expression to contradictory or complementary impulses, attitudes, etc, especially as a means of indicating detachment from a subject, theme, or emotion.' It is also described as an indirect presentation of a contradiction between an action or expression and the context in which it occurs. Irony is linked to distance and detachment. Typical thesaurus entries relating to irony include 'sarcasm, satire, sardonicism, ambiguity, equivocation, double-talk, sophistry, casuistry, double entendre,' and the thesaurus suggests related notions are under such headings as 'confusion, misinterpretation, uncertainty, detraction, disrespect, insult.'

So in the dictionary and thesaurus irony is a negative attitude on the part of a haughty ironist who looks down on those who are the butt of the ironical gesture. These 'ordinary' reference works portray irony as a surprisingly negative and judgemental act, considering the positive tone the word has in academic circles. These ordinary references also emphasise the contrast between the literal and the intended meaning of a statement, and between appearance and reality. In the more refined concepts of irony that descend from the 19th-century these features become problematic, but they do not entirely disappear.

Irony as a speech act depends on intended meaning. I say one thing and intend that you (or some bystanders) understand another. This contrast calls attention to itself. By some signal the intention is conveyed that I want you to know I am being ironic – or at least I want someone to know, not necessarily you. Undetectable irony would fail; a hoax is not irony.

Notice that since successful irony demands a signal that my words are to be taken ironically, the signal itself must be non-ironic, on pain of an infinite regress. There must be a possibility that the audience can compare the literal meaning to the ironic meaning. If all acts of communication are ironic, then none are.

This does not preclude my being ironic about the *platform* from which I am passing my ironic judgment; it precludes that the *act* of communicating irony can be endlessly doubled on itself. Irony in the ordinary sense requires that the ironist have some higher place to stand. The later developments of irony try to abolish this requirement; I will discuss to what degree they succeed in so doing. My point here is that no matter how recondite the self-irony may become, there still must be some signal that irony is going on, and that signal cannot itself be ironical.

Irony also demands the possibility of being misunderstood by being taken literally. Part of the experience of irony is the realisation that I could have understood it too simply and missed the point. If that possibility is not acknowledged, then there would be only a one-level communication, which is sarcasm, not irony.

Irony fails if it is not understood as irony; when the context required to recognise the double communication is no longer available, the irony disappears. That context might be restricted to a select few (as are the meanings of the ironic names of characters in Plato's dialogues) or no longer available (as we might lack the context to decide whether some statement in the epic of Gilgamesh was meant ironically).

Irony can also fail by excess. Ordinary factual reports and requests are undermined if they are done with too much ironic comment. If I sense irony in your request to open the door I will be unsure whether I should open the door. Performatives, too, cannot be overly ironic. How ironically could I say 'I do' and still get married? There is a limit to how far I could engage in self-parody of the act and still accomplish it. At some point I would cease being a groom and become someone putting on the role of a groom, and so fail to promise or marry. Yet works of art are more resilient, and can comment ironically on their own happening to almost unlimited degrees without vitiating their performance.

Italo Calvino's *If on a Winter's Night a Traveler* (1981) can overload and multiply self-referential narrative in a manner that can be called ironic, without ceasing to be a novel. Charles Moore's Piazza d'Italia in New Orleans can ironically overload and multiply references to its own assertions of Italian identity and festive character and still be a successful public space. But there are some limits: a house will not succeed as a house if its roof makes ironic and self-referential gestures about shelter that do not actually keep out the rain.

Irony can also fail through repetition, as the ironic gesture becomes standardised. What is the irony equivalent of dead metaphor? Some metaphors are living, some have grown stale, some have disappeared and become only another 'literal' meaning of the word. As Ricoeur says, in the dictionary there are no metaphors, only multiple meanings. Can there be ironies in the dictionary? A dead irony would be one that has become sarcasm. In sarcasm there is no intended possibility of missing the meaning. So it loses 'the curious special feeling of paradox, of the ambivalent and the ambiguous, of the impossible made actual, of a double contradictory reality'. (Muecke 1985) It ceases to be irony and becomes direct attack. Ironic gestures degrade with time; they need to be renewed; hence ironic art is driven to extremes.

Irony in the judgemental sense demands distance and double reference. The ironist refuses to be simply identified with a straightforward meaning. 'There is more to me and to what I say than the literal meaning of my words. I use this code and know it as a code. I see further; I am not just blindly following rules that are immediately one with my consciousness. I know this and you know it too.' There is detachment, and a put-down. Other types of irony keep the distance but are less judgemental. On the other hand, there are kinds of distance and complexities of reference that are not irony. For instance, play suggests a motion that is freed from strictures or rules but is not standing off and putting them down. Play has no other place to stand. Self-reflection involves a double awareness, but not necessarily the distance that brings criticism. Self-reflective persons recognise their codes and languages, but self-reflection has no particular tone; it makes possible a variety of attitudes and judgments. One such attitude would be self-consciousness in the sense of an uneasy awareness of one's own actions that gets in the way of their successful performance. This disquieted self-consciousness need not be ironic.

The most prominent of irony's cousins is parody. Parody demands some shared community understanding to begin with, as well as some signal that parody is being performed. But parody can take that community in at least two directions. As a kind of bitter satire, parody can be a weapon used by one group against another to create divisions within a community. Or it can be a playful affirmation of community. Consider, for example, the parody of medieval liturgy and theology in the Carmina Burana drinking song *In taberna quando sumus*, or the political parody of television's Saturday Night Live. In this situation we stand together as members of a community; a distance is created so that we can look at ourselves, but it does not create a superior position for some of us to occupy.

Much of what goes by the name of postmodern irony tries to be parody of this latter sort, though often it remains on the level of judgemental irony. In particular, postmodern architectural irony often ends up reaffirming the dexterous superiority of the distanced architect who has dropped by to learn a bit of the natives' language.

There are many kinds of double reference and self-awareness. Too many critics and philosophers class every kind of doubling as irony. This collapses a wide variety of attitudes and stances into one opposition between simple inhabitation and ironic distance. The result in architectural criticism has been to run together wit, humour, parody, playfulness, self-awareness, self-consciousness, irony, and the like. But then, to the extent that irony carries connotations of superior judgment, conflating all modes of double reference with irony may lead to begging major questions about the ways of living and building in our multiple world. If by definition we must be either simple-minded or ironic, the choice is obvious. Are there other forms of irony which are not caught in the blunt opposition between premodern enclosure and modern distance?

Romantic Irony

Muecke distinguishes two types of irony: closed and open. Closed irony comes about when the ironist stands within one set of beliefs and pretends ironically to hold a rival set. For example, members of one religion or political party might make ironic use of the beliefs of another. The politician may also state his own beliefs ironically, but this is done on the basis of still other, perhaps more general, beliefs that are not ironised. In contrast, what Muecke calls open irony occurs when the ironist has no particular beliefs at all to share, but wishes to be ironical about simple believers of any stripe. This irony attacks not so much the content as the act of believing. Does it still presuppose a superior position?

Renan called irony 'the act of the master by which the human spirit establishes its superiority over the world.' That superiority can be established in many ways, and there has been a steady growth in the abstractness of the platform from which irony can be exercised. Consider Voltaire, who in *Candide* and elsewhere used irony as a weapon. He had fairly straightforward beliefs of his own, but there was something about his beliefs that made them particularly apt for ironic moves. The Enlightenment critical intellect could look down on religious and political fundamentalisms from a position of relative universality; his allegiance to reason did not involve any particular substantive commitments to tradition except those demanded by the law of nature. This gave him room to manoeuvre in ironic ways, pillorying the simple faith of those dogmatists who had not attained his more universal point of view.

In the next century the same manoeuvre would be performed on Voltaire's own beliefs, first by Kant's refinement of the Enlightenment that reduced natural law to the formal demands of practical reason, and then by a series of modern ironists who saw the Enlightenment (and also Kant) as involving simple-minded commitments that could be ironically transcended by developing even more refined theories of the self and its relation to the world.

The usual authority cited for this more general irony is Friedrich Schlegel. His is often called 'romantic irony,' but Schlegel never used that term except in personal notes. He sought for an ironic attitude embodied in an art that expressed the contradictions of our situation. A commitment to reason is only one aspect that needs to be put in ironic contrast with its opposite, the boundless energy of the universe.

> It is equally fatal for the mind to have a system and to have none. It will simply have to decide to combine the two.

> Everything should be playful and serious, guilelessly open and deeply hidden . . . perfectly instinctive and perfectly conscious . . . (Art should) contain and arouse a feeling of indissoluble antagonism between the absolute and the relative, between the impossibility and the necessity of complete communication.

It is not true that this kind of irony avoids basing itself on a particular set of beliefs. Schlegel's work involves an explicit metaphysics and epistemology drawn from the philosophy of his day. According to this view we are finite beings faced with an infinite universe where nature is overflowing with forms in an infinite process of creation and destruction. Our concepts try to fix the flow because we cannot live without creating fixed objects, but we are never completely successful. We cannot reconcile subject and object, feeling and form, art and life. So Schlegel relies on a non-ironic, metaphysical description of the world and of the process of having beliefs.

Hegel pointed out that romantic irony takes its stand on self-consciousness as a process that is aware of its own form and of its movement beyond all definite content. Such irony affirms the value (or at least the inevitability) of this formally described movement of transcending whatever is given in experience. Hegel finds many problems with this view, not least with its immediate separation of form and content. But what is important for our purposes is his point that the romantic ironist does have a place to stand, a place described by straightforward philosophy of nature and subjectivity.

Deconstructive Irony

In our century we go one better than the romantics by finding an ironic stance from which the romantic theories of nature and knowledge can themselves be seen as simple beliefs subject to ironic qualification. Romantic irony depended on oppositions between the boundlessness of feeling and the restrictive necessity of form, between the ideal of communication and its inevitable frustration, and so on. Twentieth century irony has tried to add another dimension: the ideals of perfection and communication implicit at the positive poles of those oppositions must themselves be held ironically. It is not merely their frustration that we must live with, but an inherent rot at the core of the ideals themselves. We move here into deconstructive attacks on the elements constitutive of the theory of romantic irony.

This latest ironic mode does not depend on a theory about the world or about the relation between subject and object. But does this irony manage to avoid having a platform from which to judge? In many cases this is provided by a theory of the relations of signifier and signified, or of the conditions for identity.

The problem faced by deconstructive thinkers who emphasise irony is that they attack distinctions that seem constitutive of the notion of irony. We have already seen how dependent everyday irony is on the notion of intended meaning, which is a frequent target of the newest criticism. Similarly, that irony enacts some version of the distinction between appearance and reality. One thing appears to be meant, another is really meant. Romantic irony also depends on this distinction. The beliefs that seem so firm to the simple consciousness reveal their real status to the ironist.

This suggests that if we take seriously deconstructive doubts about the distinction between appearance and reality, or about the notion of intended meaning, or about the possibility of complete self-reflection or of literal meaning, we should be careful if we use 'irony' to name the result, especially if that result is declared to be universal, since irony in the ordinary sense only exists by contrast with non-ironic communication.

There is a way to make the platform from which deconstructive irony is performed *almost* disappear, but doing so demands a complex strategy. If we are to be ironic about all simple beliefs and all straightforward identities, without ourselves professing some simple meta-beliefs, we must give up metaphysical and psychological platforms. Even semiotics must go. If there are universal claims that allow our irony, they must be quasi-transcendental ones. They cease to be particular beliefs, if they can be shown to be conditions for the possibility of any belief whatsoever. Inescapable and necessary, they would provide a universally applicable but formally defined place to stand. But these are not to be the formal and synthesizing conditions one might find in Kant. They will be Derrida's *différance* and its cousins. Because of their peculiar character, these conditions cannot really be taken as forming a unified position. They qualify their own enunciation. They involve and enact difference, deferring the lack of centre or whole. Taken in themselves they make no whole, they form no immediate or mediated totality; as the conditions for grasping anything as unified and for relying on anything as a place to stand, they cannot be so grasped or used as a foundation. They provide no first or last word, but they do still provide something the ironist knows and the ordinary mortal does not.

The effect is a position that affirms and denies itself as a 'position.' Through doubling and deferred self-reference this comes close to what Muecke calls open irony, though it still depends on some universal gambits, qualified and undercut as these may be.

However, some writing labeled deconstructive also promotes immersion in the flux of life beyond stable identities and fixed oppositions; this brings back a metaphysics similar to that of the romantic ironists. Such writing is caught in the same tension as was Nietzsche, between the critique of knowledge and the desire to give us knowledge about a life that escapes concepts and critique. And, as in Nietzsche, the solution can only be in indirect communication. But is all indirect communication to be called irony?

Still, even if so far successful, deconstructive irony runs up against a problem that also infected romantic irony. As theories these do not do justice to the *location* of the ironic move. All sets of contrasts that produce meaning have the slipperiness and self-undermining that deconstruction can show. It makes no difference where we start. Hegel pointed out that the theory of romantic irony treats our finitude in general but does not look at our finite location in particular. Since all particular and determined forms of belief or life express the same ironic impossibility of their achieving the fixity and definitiveness they claim, any belief or way of life can be treated as ironic. But this can be turned around: no account can be provided for the appropriateness of the choice of certain beliefs or ways of life over others. Insofar as the irony relies upon general claims about the nature of language and truth, its point can be made from anywhere.

Thus the ironic move risks becoming a gesture that neutralises itself by its very ubiquitousness. All texts and all forms have the same irony. Demonstrations of this self-transgressing quality of all texts, using any present text as an example, can become as repetitious as appeals to original sin, and as unhelpful in dealing with particular cases in their particularity.

There is one more step to take. Can irony be freed from notions such as intended meaning and the distinction between appearance and reality? To do so would be to arrive at irony as indeterminacy and undecidability. 'The old definition of irony – saying one thing and meaning another – is superseded; irony is saying something in a way that activates not one but an endless series of subversive interpretations.' (Muecke 1985)

I am sceptical of extreme claims about undecidability, because our social practices do fix accepted meanings. We stop at the red light, understand the directions for the microwave oven, recognise the entrance to the building, comprehend the general point of the classical columns on the courthouse, and so on. What our practices cannot do is limit meaning to these accepted contours, either now or in the future. We can live with the awareness of this lack of security. Such life can be conveyed only by indirect communication (or in the act of metaphoric innovation). If we call this indirect communication irony, it can indeed be quite different from judgemental irony.

The deconstructive thought that emphasises undecidability finds irony not in the contrast of two fixed meanings, but in the contrast between the attempt to fix meaning and the impossibility of that attempt. But even this irony can be haughty or humble. It can preen itself on a platform from which it looks down on those who do not understand or who fear the openness of all systems of meaning. Or it can acknowledge that we are all in it together, in a spaciousness which, while it is no longer dominated by the old unities, does not set itself up against them.

What often gets lost is the quiet spaciousness involved in belonging somewhere. There is a way of not taking our beliefs and location too simply that is not itself the result of another level of meta-theory providing yet one more place to stand. I am not speaking of a doctrine but of an awareness of how we inhabit doctrines, a wry acknowledgment of our fragilities that affirms togetherness rather than superiority. This comes from that motion and spacing which is a condition of our inhabiting any system of meaning or practice. In philosophical and critical discourse this keeps getting twisted into something else, something that embodies hierarchy and superiority.

This is not an exercise of cognitive or valuation mastery. It offers no solid critique, except to surround any claims to solidity. Perhaps it ought not be called by the name of irony, for it is a species of compassion. But if we will use the term, perhaps we should qualify it as humble irony. The accomplishment here is one Nietzsche demanded but seldom achieved: to purge ourselves of resentment. Can we purge irony of resentment and the desire for a higher point of view than the naïve simple believer? What would irony be like if it were more play than judgment?

Architectural Irony

Postmodern architecture does not usually succeed at these refined forms of irony considered in the last section. But then, buildings have not usually been thought of as ironic at all. Even now we do not find much irony in the earnest buildings of masters like Frank Lloyd Wright or Mies van der Rohe. Ironic distance or play is the last thing Wright has in mind; he wants to convert us. Much of the history of architecture is about public buildings, and buildings meant to celebrate community values are seldom intentionally ironic; think, for example, of courthouses and the ubiquitous memorials to the American Civil War dead.

Architecture may seem less equipped for irony than the other arts. It is probably true that architecture has the greatest proportion of masterpieces that contain little or no irony. But this overlooks that there are many kinds of doubling that are not ironical. Buildings can avoid single-mindedness in their presentation and still be non-ironic in the sense that they do not stand detached from their world and announce self-consciously 'we are not wholly involved in this game we play.' A pyramid may be simple, but Chartres is not, even though neither is outstandingly ironic. Chartres takes up and extends current conceptions and values in the direction valued by the Chartres school of medieval theology; the building does not simply ratify what is already current.

What is important is not the immediacy of architectural form but the relation of the building to its world. That relation does not have to be the straight affirmation typical of American Civil War monuments. Think about some recent Vietnam War memorials; they are not ironic, but neither are they simply affirmative. Blatant incongruity and parody are alive in postmodern architecture. And they are fragile; parody and self-parody have little staying power. As the context changes, buildings outlive the irony they were meant to have. A building may be carefully designed with ironic references, perhaps in a way that subtly undercuts the authority that ordered the building for its own glory. As time passes, the building gathers its own immediate identity. Parody depends on shared reference to the style or action being parodied. With its intended contrast forgotten or ignored, today's intentional parody can be tomorrow's dull design, or worse, it may end up as an example of that which it parodies. Parody and irony can be as frail as architectural citations, which are often not lived as such by the ordinary users of the building.

It is also possible for a text or a building to become ironic even if it was not 'intended' that way. Such ironical rereading still demands a double level with reference to context. We cannot deal with the classical orders as if they stood only in the set of contrasts described by Vitruvius. In the case of this rereading no signal may be given by the, work itself, but something happens in a changed context that allows irony. No text or building possesses its form all to itself; as context changes, the form of the work changes; the possibility of irony cannot be blocked any more than can the possibility of new metaphors and multiple readings. In this sense irony is a permanent possibility, but it is not permanently available, since it depends on contrasts which can never be completely held within the work itself. To imagine that irony is always waiting to be revealed is to fall into modernist illusions about the completeness and independence of the aesthetic object.

As they proclaim an irony of play and ambiguity, most postmodern architects stand on non-ironic theories about the nature of architectural communication and meaning. Jencks speaks of our strong eclecticism as based on a knowledge of semiotics. Moore and Graves discourse on the way architecture means. In so doing they rejoin the modern movement, which also claimed to work from universal theories about architectural meaning. Except in some recent deconstructive projects, we do not see in architecture the self-undermining irony found in recent literature and criticism.

The postmoderns stand with the moderns against the presumed simple inhabitation of our ancestors. What moderns and postmoderns share is a distance due to self-awareness. We are told that our eyes have been opened and it is impossible to live within one style or vocabulary. When we use a style we need to signal this awareness by an ironic move.

Vitruvius certainly was aware of the rules for classical architecture and he could contrast it with other modes of building used, say, in Egypt. What he did not do was refer to it as a style. Styles come in the plural; the notion indicates that there are many styles available compared to the one we choose or are given. Theories of appropriate and natural styles are designed to overcome the distance created by the very use of the notion of style.

People have always known that others built differently; but we are told that they did not always see these different ways as a palette of styles from which they might choose. They just built the way people did in their community. We tell ourselves that from the Renaissance on, builders developed a more open attitude that led to a swifter pace of change, culminating in the eclecticism of the 19th-century, which seems to have returned today. This story neglects the mutual influences and metaphoric combinations that have gone on at a slow pace throughout history. But whether or not it is a new phenomenon, the distance implicit in the notion of style is not the same as irony.

One way to make irony out of that distance is to add some platform from which the ironist can pass judgments. Another way is what I have called humble irony. Humble irony qualifies the inhabitation of particular places. It is not an affirmation of a universal theory, though we recognise in it a universal condition. We can enact our inhabitation in ways that convey our awareness of its fragility. For example, if we create or find new meanings and let them work as new, the sidelong awareness of contingency and fragility is signalled by the act of changing or blending the vocabulary. This is not done from some distanced survey but on the spot, extending the field as we walk over the old borders. That act is enough to remind us of our finitude; we do not need signs with Day-Glo colours.

In architecture, traditional vocabularies might be used and metaphorically changed in ways that affirm a solidarity that is not that of shared immediate belief, a solidarity that remains comfortable with future reinterpretation. There is room for buildings that are neither naïve celebrations nor elitist games. Often, though, ironic use of traditional motifs becomes a doubly coded way of indicating how much more the architect knows. Postmodern buildings may avoid the modern movement's antagonism for the past, but they have a harder time avoiding the avant-garde's resentment for the bourgeoisie.

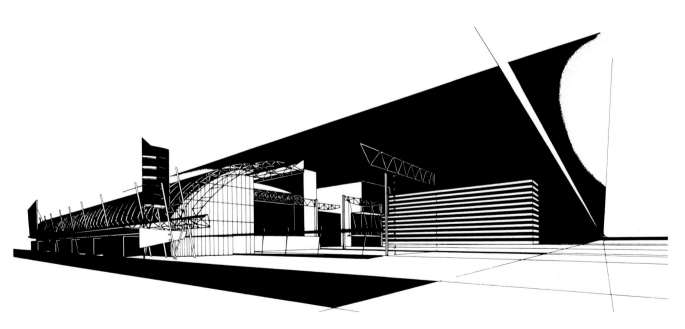

BERNARD TSCHUMI, NATIONAL THEATRE, TOKYO

———————— * ————————

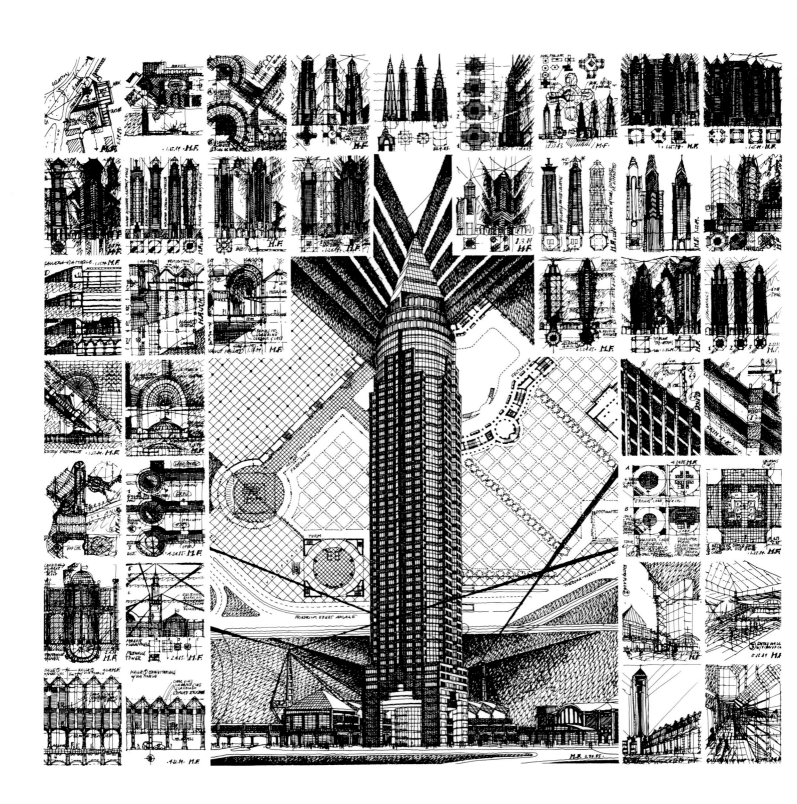

HELMET JAHN, MESSE TOWER, FRANKFURT

PHILIP COOKE
BACK TO THE FUTURE

It was in the urban landscapes of large American and European cities that postmodernism first imprinted itself upon the gaze of the ordinary public. In the late 1970s, new styles of architecture appeared, apparently rejecting the austerity of modernism by including ornamentation, colour (of a pastel rather than a primary kind) and heterogeneous forms such as the barrel-vaulted glass atrium or the classical

façade with pitched roof, in place of the uniform cubes of late modernism. By the late 1980s postmodern architecture consisted of a number of different styles, some of which could even be seen to be obvious continuations of modernism, notably the 'high-tech' buildings of Norman Foster, especially his Hong Kong & Shanghai Bank, and Richard Rogers, whose Lloyds' Insurance building in the City of London celebrated, as did Foster's, the modernist idea that function should not only determine form but that it should pervade its every visible facet.

Other architects whose work has been described as postmodern, such as Charles Moore, Michael Graves, Helmut Jahn, Leon Krier, Ricardo Bofill, Aldo Rossi and the later designs of Philip Johnson, amongst many, have rejected Mies van der Rohe's thesis that 'Less is more,' the clarion call of modernism, and decided that pure form is not enough. Rossi and Krier's work has been described as 'neo-rationalist,' Moore's and Bofill's as 'neo-classicist,' Graves' and Johnson's as 'historicist,' while Jahn's glass and steel towers both echo modernist uses of material and the revival of typical early modern American skyscrapers, themselves often neo-gothic in inspiration. It is strange, therefore, that criticism has frequently been directed at postmodern architecture because of its lack of aesthetic reference to historical forms of building and design. It is said, particularly by Frederic Jameson, that postmodern architecture is merely pastiche, playful, not serious, populist and marks a departure from the higher ideals to which modernism, through its aesthetic connections with the theory of proportion in classical architecture, aspired. This criticism, it is worth adding, has also been made of postmodern fiction, by Charles Newman and others though it hardly stands close scrutiny given the often grand historical sweep which such texts as those of García Marquéz, Salman Rushdie and Italo Calvino display.

Nevertheless, it is a charge worth exploring, since it is clear that the way historical reference is incorporated in postmodern architecture is very different from that represented in modernist stylistics. Perhaps the key characteristics of postmodern architecture, consistent with postmodernism in other fields, is that it is 'double-coded.' Whereas modernist architecture communicated with the past and present by means of a code that was hermetically sealed to all who were not privileged members of the professional elite who could be expected to know or understand what was going on, postmodern architecture both does that same thing, in a more obvious and specific way, and communicates directly, often with local relevance, to the ordinary public who live with its results. In this sense postmodern architecture can often be irreverent in the way that it uses and combines motifs from the past. Such ironies are equally meant to appeal to the public and professional audience alike. This is where postmodernism differs significantly from the po-faced anti-modernism of Quinlan Terry and the Prince of Wales. Their classicism is undiluted revivalism intended to be revered as much as enjoyed.

We can explore the historical dimension in three subplanes through examining three instances of postmodern architecture that range from the macro to the micro scales. The first example is Ricardo Bofill's monumental constructions as exemplified in the French new town of St-Quentinen-Yvelines near Paris and in the Mediterranean city of Montpellier. Both are large-scale public sector housing schemes, a fact which marks Bofill's work thus far as somewhat distinct from the office buildings or museums of which much postmodern architecture seems presently to consist. Bofill builds high-rise architecture of a scale more typical of the late modernist housing schemes which pioneered the style. However, the design of the schemes themselves seems to owe more to Cecil B. de Mille or at least Caesar's Rome, than to Le Corbusier. In St-Quentin the monumental slabs are set in a lake and either side of the apartment windows are set series of gigantic classical pillars, much greater in scale than those ever built in Athens, Rome or even 19th-century New York, Paris or London.

In Montpellier, the same monumental style is repeated except on a more limited scale. The Antigone, as his development is named, flows from the modernist Polygon retail and office centre located at the open end of what has been turned into a vast, *fin de siècle* piazza complete with revivalist fountain and refurbished opera house. Antigone itself consists of two large, circular piazzas, linked by a 'neck' from the side of which entry is made into the vast enclosed spaces. Again, the housing is multi-storey and the main projecting points where curve meets line are set off by the enormous classical pillars. Within the piazzas, separating off pedestrianised circulation space from relaxation space are pedimented arches, more decorative than functional. The whole edifice is built of golden, prefabricated cement panels redolent in colour and texture of Cotswold stone.

Bofill's designs are slightly unnerving in that they can at first seem to echo the architecture of less elevated historical episodes such as Mussolini's Rome. But there is less quasi-modern stylisation, and more, albeit prefabricated, attention to social enclosure than to triumph in the architecture. The buildings convey a sense both of providing secure, pleasant, traffic-free living space and of an ironic representation of the particular local history of these French cities as parts of the Romanised empire. Moreover, by providing such palatial-looking accommodation (inside, the apartments are cramped functional-modern) for public sector tenants the point is made that in the contemporary period there is no need for palaces only to be associated with the luxury housing of the rich. That class transgression and the care with which the open space, shopping and drinking amenities have been incorporated into the overall design suggest an improvement albeit idiosyncratic, on the alienating products of modernist mass housing policy.

Philip Johnson's AT&T Building in Manhattan is also typically monumental, though in this case a single tower. Johnson, who was a disciple of Le Corbusier, has adapted his late modernist steel and glass cubism by changing the facing material to the postmodernist pastel of polished pink granite, then topping the whole edifice off with a Chippendale broken pediment. This joke, for it is too blatant an act to be considered irony or even parody, has caused outrage because of its apparent meaninglessness and egotism. But it deflects attention from two more positive features of postmodernism. First, it lessens the distance, at least symbolically, between the higher reaches of aesthetic professionalism and the man or woman in the street, each of whom may reflect on the similarity between the building and the tallboy in auntie's bedroom. But secondly, and more importantly, the design incorporates a public plaza which invites the passer-by into the building, to treat it, if only during the working day, as a space for sociability, unlike its modernist forebears. Foster's bank building in Hong Kong does the same in opening up a shared space through which the public is encouraged to pass to a nearby park. Is this just corporate capitalism pretending to be friendly? Perhaps. But in the process a little of the alienation created by modernist exclusiveness is undermined.

The micro-scale example of postmodern historicity is Charles Moore's Piazza d'Italia in New Orleans. This is precisely a local cultural artefact in that it is simply an open public arena on a small scale built in and for the Italian community in the city. It is a circular piazza, set in the grid of a streetblock, surrounded by various motifs from the distant and not so distant past. Classical arches, a podium, Latin inscriptions, a Fontana de Trevi and black and white contrasts are reminiscent of the Gothic Duomo of Florence or Siena. Because the Italian community of the city is predominantly Sicilian in origin, the concentric circles of the piazza are transected by a map of Italy with Sicily in the centre. There is illusion where a column turns into a fountain, and in the use of materials which, despite appearances, are mass-produced cement and steel, and the ornamentation has the look not of the craftsmans effort but of the factory-produced artefact. Despite its obviousness, or more likely because of it, the construction works and is locally popular through its capacity to echo and reproduce in a new-old form the local identity of those uprooted by the global forces of modernity. Once again the style is inclusive, democratic and historicist, but in ways that have meaning for the residents of the locality.

These themes also underlie the architectural philosophies of the neo-rationalists Aldo Rossi and Leon Krier. They have reacted against Le Corbusier's injuction to 'kill the street' by rethinking the elements of the pre-modern city, destroyed under the modernist regime, in terms of basic forms and functions. The street, the open space and the different types of buildings, domestic, official, commercial and so on constitute the elements which they have sought to reintegrate. This reworking of classical motifs has led Krier to design schemes which link functions such as the public and the private through reviving the street, the square, the monumental focusing point. Designs for private or public housing include the street, not necessarily as a grid-like dividing device but a diagonal, integrating space of flows in layouts which respect human scale. There is, in this architecture, some danger of tipping over into reactionary anti-modernism but thus far this pitfall seems to have been avoided, not least by the measure of irony and parody of the past which their designs continue to display.

Sometimes the ironic playfulness of postmodern architecture tips over in the other direction, back to a new kind of elitism. This is a danger with which Michael Graves seems to have flirted unsuccessfully. As Linda Hutcheon puts it in discussing his (unbuilt) amber, turquoise and magenta Fargo-Moorhead Cultural Bridge between North Dakota and Minnesota, drawing on the analysis of the architectural historian Charles Jencks:

Jencks has trouble dealing . . . with its admitted echoes of Ledoux, Castle Howard, Serharia, Wilson's architecture at Kew, Asplund, Borromini and others . . . of modernist concrete construction, of mannerist broken pediments, and of cubist colours. Jencks acknowledges that the meaning of these historical references would likely be lost on the average citizen of the American mid-west.

This seems to be an example of the architect's wish to display his learning to the profession, and also to out-perform his later masterpieces (as at Portland, Oregon, in the chocolate-box of a public facilities building, decorated with a bronze bust of 'Portlandia,' second only in scale to the Statue of Liberty), rather than speak democratically to the local citizenry.

So, postmodernism in architecture is as prone as postmodern fiction to the dangers of incomprehensibility, but neither at their best suffer from this problem as much as the avowedly elitist products of hermetic late modernism. Postmodernism as built form is conscious of the need to close the gap between high and low culture, to communicate in symbols which the untutored citizen may be better able to understand and enjoy and, above all, to replace the homogeneous universality of modernist discourse with a more heterogeneous, locally sensitive and inclusive language which entertains as it parodies the pretensions of the past.

The Critique of Postmodernism

Perhaps surprisingly, given what has been said about the elements of subversion, irreverence, parody and sensitivity to locality, even a degree of popular democracy, that are contained within the postmodern critique, it has received its sternest criticisms from Marxist aestheticians. The foremost among these has been Frederic Jameson. Jameson sees postmodernism in all its forms; poetry, fiction, architecture, music and the visual arts, as the cultural correlate of the latest stage in the development of capitalism, the capitalism of pure consumption, the onset of consumer society. This society is advanced, hyper-modern, postindustrial, media-dominated, given to indulging in spectacle, dominated by multinational capital. Its two most significant features are its preference for pastiche and a schizophrenic disposition.

By pastiche, Jameson means the taking of original styles and imitating or mimicking them in the absence of some sense of respect for them. Pastiche, Jameson says, is humourless because it has lost touch with the universal norms by means of which artists or satirists justify picking upon particular styles to ridicule. In the modernist era there were such norms even though the styles could be diverse and original. But because of that originality, which also conveyed a sense of authenticity, the satirist remained in touch with the norms by which the judgement of authenticity had been made. Amongst the most important of such norms was the concept of the authentic, creative individual. Pastiche signifies that individualism of that kind is dead for the reasons that have been discussed already. The critique of subjectivity as produced by Foucault; the idea that only texts matter (and are in any case the product of many texts shimmering off each other, after Derrida); and the apocalyptic notion of the death of the subject proposed by those, such as Jean Baudrillard, who see us all as slaves to the power of mass-media – all these have contributed to a strange devaluing of the subject, in which condition pastiche thrives.

Moreover, as Jameson puts it, in seeking to explain the emergence of pastiche as a kind of sub-aesthetic:

There is another sense in which the writers and artists of the present will no longer be able to invent new styles and worlds – they've already been invented; only a limited number of combinations are possible; the most unique ones have been thought of already. So the weight of the whole modernist aesthetic tradition – now dead – also 'weighs like a nightmare on the brains of the living,' as Marx said in another context.

So art becomes artifice, the endless recycling of the styles of the past. Hence, the inflated market for nostalgia and the reinterpretation of the past in fiction, film, art and architecture, even in rock music, once the province of a kind of insurgent originality. Old plots, like old songs or themes are plagiarised unashamedly, given an archaic feel even when the setting may be a contemporary one. Consumer capitalism seems to have robbed contemporary culture of the capacity to produce original statements. Worse than that, its artefacts confine us, exclude us, disorient us as in the examples Jameson gives of the postmodern hotels and shopping plazas which resist decoding, save only to project an image of mindless consumption upon our brains.

The schizophrenic aspect that Jameson sees in postmodernism derives from what he calls the disappearance of a sense of history. The cultural recycling places us in a permanent present of changing images supplied by the mass-media, the fashion industry, advertising, changes in style. This is something akin to the experience of the schizophrenic patient who suffers a loss of the integrated view of the self as having a past, present and future, and a sense of detachment from reality.

Because of this fragmentation of time, exemplified in the pervasiveness of such ideas as 'built-in obsolescence' and 'replacement buying' which the communications industries project as the motive force of consumer society, its members begin to experience a kind of historical amnesia. We forget the past and accept its reproduction in various pre-packaged forms of nostalgia. In that process lies the danger – Jameson leaves his options open at this point – that postmodernism means passive compliance with this dominating consumer society. Unlike modernism which produced culturally dissonant, even shocking subversions of and oppositions to the norms of conventional bourgeois society, postmodernism, for Jameson, lacks this sense of resistance.

To some extent, these arguments have been anticipated in the preceding discussion. It is important, as was noted in the assessment of postmodernist fiction and architecture, to recognize that there is some basis for Jameson's strictures. Postmodernism can seem, as Jameson and others have said elsewhere, depthless, eclectic and disoriented. Moreover, in architecture especially, it seems highly complicit with the power structure of consumer society. Unquestionably, many postmodern buildings and even wider segments of the urban landscape such as the waterfront developments that have become commonplace in large cities, cater to the tastes and lifestyles of the rich and famous. Corporate capital was amongst the earliest purchasers of the fashionably new styles. And although it is important not to overlook the role of the public sector in commissioning the work of some of the leading newer architects such as Bofill, Graves, Moore and Krier, it can still, as a critic in the *Architectural Review* put it, 'look like little more than the pretty plaything of rampant capitalism.'

It is not clear why this should surprise the critics. Corporate capital quickly appropriated virtually every fashionable new architectural style that preceded postmodern architecture. It is difficult to see why postmodernism should be any different. In this respect it can be argued that these styles are no more or less complicit with the values of the corporate elite than any other.

But, to return to the issue Jameson raises regarding the pastiche-like quality of postmodern aesthetic forms, it is instructive to consider the distinction he makes between parody (good) and pastiche (bad). In a lengthy discussion of the concept of parody Linda Hutcheon argues that its meaning is more ambiguous than Jameson allows. While he defines it solely as satirical or ridiculing imitation, she points out that the root of the word in the Greek *para* gives it the double meaning both of 'against' and also 'beside.' On this basis, postmodernism is engaged in parody rather than pastiche because it involves critical, often ironic reinterpretation of standard aesthetic norms, pointing to differences but remaining within or beside the tradition. One of the more common ironic references is towards modernism's loss of touch with the local and popular levels of aesthetic appreciation.

The other dimension of Jameson's critique – namely that postmodernism marks a loss of historical reference, a schizophrenic problem of identity in relation to time, a situation of time being a permanently recycled sense of the present – seems equally unfounded when consideration is given to the way that historical reference infuses large areas of postmodern aesthetics. Moreover, if the second meaning of the concept of parody is deployed it is much harder to argue as Jameson does that postmodernism represents a kind of neutral. untethered relationship to the canon of norms or aesthetic regime that developed with modernism's challenge to classical aesthetics. There are striking similarities between modernism's Janus-face, looking backwards in order to move forward, and that of postmodernism in which there is, if anything, a stronger desire to vault backwards over the austere hermeticism of the late modern era in order to move forward into a renewed, more accessible aesthetic regime.

In conclusion, therefore, these two main critical thrusts, around which other critical charges have accreted, are over-exaggerated. They fail to recognize the ambiguity in postmodern art and architecture between working within the cultural and wider socio-economic system and simultaneously subverting aspects of it. Irony is mistaken for oppositionism and local sensitivity – where it exists – for a rejection of universal and transcendent norms. Even Jameson does not deny that progressive cultural and social insights and practices can arise from within the postmodern perspective. Perhaps undue attention has been paid to postmodernism's historical coincidence with the rise of neoconservative politics and the crisis of institutions such as the Keynesian welfare state and Fordist modes of regulation and forms of accumulation. The undoubted reductionism in Jameson's analysis – shared with other Marxist critiques such as that of Terry Eagleton, Mike Davis and others whose thoughtful commentaries have appeared in the *New Left Review* during the 1980s – is testimony to the problems of engaging in a totalising form of modern discourse. A Postmodernism critique questions precisely this monolithic, totalising perspective.

MICHAEL GRAVES, SWAN HOTEL, FLORIDA

CHARLES JENCKS
POST-MODERNISM BETWEEN KITSCH AND CULTURE

Today an architectural movement may find it easier to survive persecution than success. Widespread acceptance not only diffuses the aims of a tradition – because so many followers get them partially wrong – but it also confuses the leaders. Single-minded and strong in opposition, they lose direction when they become the focus for mass culture and adulation. They may confuse their own success with a deeper

change in society or the profession of architecture; or their message may be co-opted by large firms in a way that betrays its essential meaning. Such things had happened to Post-Modern architecture by the late 1980s as it became successful, middle-aged, part of the Establishment and taught in the academies.

Conceived as a wide language which cuts across high and low taste cultures with a double-coding that still holds the integrity of each voice, it can result in crude compromise. In the 1950s Dwight MacDonald and other literary critics damned such mixed gruel as Mid-Cult – neither high nor low culture but a parody of both. This is the constant danger for Post-Modernists in every area, especially the most commercial ones: film, TV, music, the popular novel and architecture. Always trying to reach a wider and more varied audience than that which John Barth (following Thomas Mann) calls 'the Early Christians: professional devotees of high art', Post-Modernists may be constantly tempted to simplify their message, edit out its irony and double-coding, and appeal to the largest group with the falsely consoling idea of an integrated culture.[1]

This oversimplification betrays the basic goal of the movement, which is to enhance pluralism and cultural difference. Totalisation, by contrast, was often the goal of traditional culture and Modernism, especially in the latter's Heroic Period and the 1930s. Then Walter Gropius, Mies van der Rohe, Giuseppe Terragni and Le Corbusier, among many other Modernists, made their placating overtures to the centralising states of the time – the Nazis, Fascists and Petain's government.[2] Modernists today might prefer to forget these revealing slips into compromise, especially since their movement is often portrayed as anti-Establishment and pure. But these lapses, and Nikolaus Pevsner's defense of the new architecture as 'totalitarian' (in the 1936, but not later editions of his *The Pioneers of the Modern Movement)* should make them look again. Their halo has always been a bit tarnished. The 'universalist' tendency of Modernism was always an inducement to compromise with power, and remains so today. Post-Modernists, with their theories of pluralism, have produced a new form of compromise – sending different groups or taste cultures different messages – and not trying to resolve the implications for society as a whole. To repeat: there's a downside to all traditions, especially evident when they are most successful.

Disney Gives PM the Kiss
In 1985 Michael Eisner, head of the Walt Disney empire, set up the Disney Development Corporation and decided to develop theme parks, resorts and convention hotels as an integrated package. In this he was enormously enterprising, transforming a $1 billion per year turnover into $5 billion – revenue which was mostly dependent on parks and resorts, not films.[3] Euro-Disneyland, opening in 1992 outside Paris, is a $2.3 billion, 4,800 acre resort/theme-park and what-have-you (with Grid Building by Frank Gehry, the Happy Trails Motel by Antoine Predock and other themoids by

Antoine Grumbach, Michael Graves and Robert Stern). Disney World in Florida, on 28,000 acres, is already a mega-park of specialised fun. This is perplexing. Why millions of people like to congregate together in one fantasy ghetto to undergo a strict regime of entertainment escapes me, but it's a secret on which the Disney corporation has thrived for years. The formula of controlled ride-through parks, 'theming', ersatz and mechanised experience appeals to the masses as much as it does to the multinationals, and it led to the 'crisis of Modern architecture'. Fifteen years later it struck Post-Modernism.

Robert Stern designed Michael Eisner's parents' Manhattan apartment in the early 1970s so it was perhaps predictable that Eisner would consult Stern for architectural advice. This led to a meeting with Michael Graves and the transformation of Disney, as Paul Goldberger put it, into 'the IBM of the post-modern age'.[4] Not only did this conglomerate commission well over a billion dollars of work from Post-Modern architects, but Eisner asked Graves and Stern for strategic advice in transforming his empire from what was a mass-cult enterprise – when Walt Disney died – into something more up-market. It is too soon to judge the results of this policy, which in the end will take ten years, focusing on three cities, but one can estimate the outlines through the two hotels by Michael Graves in Florida: there will be something like 18 more of these leviathans including some office buildings in the future.

The first conclusion may seem too obvious to mention, but from it everything follows: Graves' structures are big. The Swan Hotel, with its 28-ton turquoise birds, has 758 bedrooms, the Dolphin Hotel has 1,510 and together these artificial mountains cost more than a third of a billion – $375,000,000. The average huge hotel built during the London boom in the early 70s had 500 bedrooms and creates a disruption in scale and city life which amounts to the occupation of an invading army – a role tourists tend to fulfil. Here, in the reclaimed swamps of Florida, it is ironically the hotels the tourists will come to see: they are far more interesting and culturally challenging than anything to be found in the ride-through parks.

This 'entertainment architecture', as Eisner has christened the fruits of his new policy, has more references to European culture than a PhD source-spotter can find in all the Magic Kingdom. Some of it is a bit heavy, like Bernini's swans inflated nine times in volume from the old perches by the Palazzo Barberini, now to loom 47 feet above the awed hordes. The other exterior sources are more allusive – water cascade from the Villa Lante, sailboat bridge and central pyramid from Ledoux, stepped massing from Zoser's famous pyramid, and the layout from the 19th-century Ecole des Beaux-Arts. Such Euro-delights rev one up for more sourcery on the inside (13 restaurants, one themed as a fish, the next as the Palio race-course, etc). The ride-through park has now become the walk-through cafeteria with menu by Sir Bannister Fletcher: comparative Western architecture on the digestive method.

Most of these delights were run up in a year or two when Graves, like Disney, had an enormous boom. In April 1990, his office had just completed eight major projects – such as the Newark Museum Renovation at $17 million, or the Crown American Corporate Headquarters at $27 million – and had 64 more under way. Most were hotels, offices and commercial buildings, but others included five large private houses and five museums, bringing the total amount of work to over a billion dollars. Such figures may be misleading, but it is still of interest to compare them with those of Philip Johnson who, at the height of his success in 1985, had 13 mega-projects in hand and $2.5 billion worth of work.[5]

Perhaps with a hint of competitive spleen Robert Stern dubbed Graves 'the Paul Rudolph of PM', because so much of the work was signature-stamped rather than context-specific: it said more about who designed it than where it was. But closer to the mark would be 'the SOM of PM', because like this large firm, Graves churns out architecture of a generally high standard. The question then might be – 'Isn't it all really *Modern*'?

Mechanisation, quick speed of production, massive scale of building, stereotyping are all hallmarks of the Modern Movement, especially in its latest alienating phase. But the related question

one has trouble seeing them as they almost disappear in a quack of banality. Worse yet, underneath the oleaginous skin there are two extraordinary realities – a steel frame, and the plywood ribs on which the fibreglass is stuck. Here are two unpredictable and elegant deep structures which the typical Post-Modernist – Venturi, Stirling, Hollein to name the three obvious ones – would have partly revealed. This would have made the emblems both literal swans *and* beautiful diagrams which showed their internal workings. If ever there were a case for producing a multivalent symbol that would work on many levels of perception and taste, it was here with these multi-layered, but hidden structures. At 47 feet they might even have been used as habitable rooms.

Aside from their size and a few other infelicitous blotations like the turquoise sea-shells, the buildings are quite imaginative and praiseworthy. The interiors show a lighter touch than the outside, and an interesting handling of what could be called colour-field architecture. Especially successful is the long lobby of the Swan, which creates a vibrating pattern of floral lights, cut-out palms and parrot chandeliers – all against a red, white and blue backdrop. It's the kind of cheap, but convincing all-over pattern which Robert Venturi and others have been attempting for years, but never

L TO R: MICHAEL GRAVES, SWAN HOTEL, FLORIDA; NEWARK MUSEUM

also has to be asked, when it comes to designing entertainment architecture: 'How big is too big?' Here one finds divergent answers. As functioning hotels my view is that the Swan and Dolphin are not much better or worse than the average, gargantuan Sheraton which is their equal in cost and type: impersonal, efficient and bland in service. But as stage sets, which is the more proper comparison, they are on the scale of Cecil B DeMille and quite appropriate for circuses and the slaughter of the Christians. The critique might thus be one that Reyner Benham levels at the Getty Museum: 'no blood was spilled here'. Blood is no more likely to flow at the Swan or Dolphin, given the super-controlled Disney atmosphere. The problem then is less that the hotels are too big than that the everyday activity is too small. One needs grand functions for the grandiosity to feel right – something like the naval battles staged on false lakes, as the Romans and Florentines used to put on behind their similarly Herculean palazzi.

All the problems of scale, size, detailing and conception are well symbolised by the sweet little predatory birds which dominate the swamps for miles. The swans give the hotel its name, and are repeated resonantly throughout the interior. But they are so predictable in every fibreglass inch of smile and arch of neck that

achieved so successfully. Furthermore, the drama is sustained over a series of public spaces right through the corridors and into the bedrooms. The pictorial effects is as if one crossed a David Hockney with a Paul Cézanne – the Pop images of trees and beach umbrellas with the more subtle tonalities of a Provencal landscape. What one misses in photographs, but is apparent from the plans, is that Graves has become adept at pacing the sequence of classical rooms that vary in shape and size. He has understood the Beaux-Arts promenade for which he is here finding a new use and mood.

This is even more true of his renovations for the Newark Museum in New Jersey, a laborious job of shoe-horning a fine collection of mostly American art into a converted YWCA and other old buildings. Graves started talking about the project in 1967 and then designed it from 1982 to 1990, so in terms of scale and speed of production it is the opposite of his Disney work. Here the earlier small houses and the showrooms for the Sunar Corporation have paid dividends: Graves has produced one of the few really convincing buildings of Post-Modern Classicism. From the stuccoed entrance through the round, square and rectangular spaces the visitor proceeds both understanding the logic and anticipating surprise. Low and high spaces are set in subtle contrast, drawing one forward. Every so often the sudden reappearance of a dramatic skylight punctuates the sequence, reminiscent of the John Soane museum – and it's a measure of Graves' success that his building can stand up to the comparison. The Soane Museum and Soane's Dulwich Museum and Art Gallery as well as Graves' buildings are all in a restrained classicism of wall planes, skylights and slight articulations that create an ever-varying backdrop to the art. The proportion of flat surface to void reaches an optimum for a museum, and I can think of no better ratio in recent architecture, unless it is the Picasso Museum in Paris. In any case, the relation of the background building to the foreground art is as satisfying as I've found.

A consequence of the understated classicism – close to the Tuscan mode – is that it can seem an inevitable partner to the existing brick vernacular, the old YWCA, and also accept the new synthetic vernacular: the vinyl floor tiles, municipal EXIT signs and industrial sprinkling system. Such are the realities for any but the most expensive museum. In accommodating their presence in an abstract way Graves produces a double-coding that convinces one it is possible to refer both to the Age of Plastic and the ancient Greeks. Much of the collection is Yankee Neo-Classical and thus

angle of fast-build, the 64 projects under way are noteworthy because of their high average quality. This is, oddly enough, a point the Modernist Aldo van Eyck would appreciate: although the self-confessed enemy of Gravesian Post-Modernism, he does preach the 'quality of quantity' rather than the much easier quality of small-scale production. However, judged solely in these terms, those of pre-industrial handcraft, the buildings are diagrammatic.

The balance of contending judgements could continue endlessly, culminating in the Disney work itself. Looked at in terms of the corporation's past, the new 'entertainment architecture' is obviously one giant step better than Cinderella's Castle (a sugary pastiche of Ludwig II of Bavaria's pastiche of *Les Tres Riches Heures'* exaggeration of a real Gothic castle); but seen in terms of the developing Post-Modern tradition of ornament and symbolism, some of the work is regressive. This is particularly true of the Seven Dwarfs façade of the headquarters building for Disney in Burbank, California. This phase in Graves' work has been called 'hokey-tecture' because its tongue-in-cheek fakery is so knowing.[6] The attempt, as in kitsch, is to succeed through excess; but when it is this calculating and obvious, one wonders. 'I've tried to walk the line between the whimsical and the jokey', Graves has said, 'or to

MICHAEL GRAVES, DISNEY HEADQUARTERS, BURBANK, CALIFORNIA

also relates to this cultural gap. The culminating space of the museum intensifies the same duality: the 'atrium', which shoots up four stories and unites all levels in a single view, is at once spartan and grand. Industrial glazing is set against a yellowish *faux-marbre,* while the abstract pattern created by punched-out window voids has a bi-axial symmetry. The whole space has the dignity of a present-day Pantheon, created with minimalist means. The particular virtue of the space is that it affords glimpsed and framed views of what is to come, increasing the anticipation of further pleasures. In this way it is rather like the central space of the Guggenheim Museum, except that here, rectangular and semi-enclosing walls form a stable backdrop for the art.

What conclusions can one draw from this stage of Graves' career and its intersection with the fortunes of Disney? Some of his work is produced slowly and remains well-controlled, like the Newark conversion, whereas an equal amount is produced quickly, like the Momochi apartment building in Japan, a caricature of his style. Perhaps another third is both creatively integral and yet still flawed in parts, like the Youngstown Museum. This has an interesting massing that is ultimately dissatisfying because of its heavily proportioned backside and notional details. Looked at from the

navigate between the chasm ·of the cute and the abyss of easy irony'. The question is, what positive terrain exists between these four trifles?

One thinks of Mannerist and Baroque fantasies, those of Giuliano da Romano and the fountains of Rome, which had an equally explicit imagery; or the papal symbolism that dominates Catholic structures; or even iconic roadside architecture, the Hot-Dog stand. Each of these, in different ways, is equally literal with its signs – so what is it that makes them more acceptable? Perhaps craftsmanship in the first case, the actual content in the second, and the surreal brazenness of the third. In 300 years' time, might the Seven Dwarfs turn into mysterious icons?

As it is, Dopey, the central dwarf caryatid – a mere 19 foot midget – looks for the moment only like Dopey. Unlike Michael Graves' earlier sketches for sculpture – notably 'Portlandia' for the Portland Building – there is no ambiguity, abstraction and transformation of the content and image. The whole façade becomes a 'signolic', not symbolic architecture.[7] Just as the circular tempietto which surmounts the scheme is a one-liner, so too are the dwarfs – which unfortunately set the opening theme. This stereotyping is a pity because it makes one overlook the strengths of the plan and the back elevation: the latter, for instance, fully absorbs one of the hallmarks of the new Disney architecture – Mickey Mouse ears – into an interesting bay rhythm that, at the same time, turns the corner very well. The building, at these points, becomes more resonant and symbolic.

Robert Stern's work for the corporation varies more widely, from the revivalist beach resort hotel to the crazy decorated shed that is the Casting Centre for Disney, in Orlando, Florida. This latter confection has the real spirit and vulgarity of roadside architecture, it is definitely aiming at what Herbert Gans – a major theorist of Post-Modernism – would call the 'lower middle taste culture', those suburbanites who cruise the edges of Houston and Los Angeles looking for cheap real estate which still has royal pretensions. Bald-faced deceit this brazen is sublime. The diaper pattern meant to evoke the Doge's Palace and the Grand Canal has, indeed, Gothicesque windows, but like the airfoil entrance canopy [sic], it belongs very much in The Age of Metal. Two little golden peaked finials (gratis Aldo Rossi) hold this airplane wing in place, while a truly grotesque lantern giggles between them.

Just so no one could possibly take any of this seriously, the images are collaged out of phase and their flat insubstantiality is exaggerated by paper-thin layering. Blue Mickey Mouse ears further punctuate the pretence, and Mickey Mouse's head is, appropriately enough, empty – the perfect visual void. (One is reminded here of Stern's masterful satire of the Best discount store and its caryatids with their empty heads shaped like TV sets.)

The view from the roadside spells C A S T I N G in giant gilt letters. One goes into this decorated shed to get a job as an imagineer, or some other engineer of fantasy, and is delighted to find the Disney icons played with as well as put on pedestals. Through his shifts in scale and violent confrontations of good and bad taste, through his collage of genres, Stern, of all the architects, has come closest to re-using the Disney iconography for his own whimsical purposes.

At this stage of incompletion, the Disney work still cannot be judged as a whole, nor can its effects on Post-Modernism be gauged. Some Post-Modernists such as James Stirling have declined Disney commissions because, as he said: 'To me [the theme idea] seems demeaning and trivial and somehow not profound or important. It's overly commercial. In England, we're subjected to it in a gross way – the parading of the guards, the dressing up at the Tower of London, and Madame Tussaud's. Maybe we invented the bloody thing'.[8] Robert Venturi, Charles Moore, Aldo Rossi, Hans Hollein have all been considered for jobs, and may still get them; Arata Isozaki is producing the 'Time Building' in Florida – what looks to be the most dignified and abstractly themed structure so far. Many more Post-Modern architects are at work, so the tradition is now deeply involved with, and implicated in, the fortunes of Disney. Michael Graves and Robert Stern contend, as do others who are at work here, that entertainment architecture should not be judged by the same canons as serious work, but rather on a populist level: whether people like it; whether, in Stern's laconic, Warholian words, 'Disney is fun'.[9]

So far their schemes are successful in these restricted terms – no small endeavour – but questionable on more ambitious levels. If so many Post-Modernists had not been commissioned at once, for so many expensive and visible jobs; if the Disney empire had not turned their change of style into a media event and dominated the Sunday supplements; if Post-Modernism were not at the same time so concerned with the incorporation of high and low tastes and symbolism, then I wouldn't waste my time writing about it, and would accept Stern's singular canon of judgement. As it is, by historic accident the Walt Disney world happened to be changing its look and market niche just at the moment when Post-Modernism was most fashionable and vulnerable, and so their fortunes crossed. Whether in the end this will be seen as the kiss of life, or death, for

the PM movement remains open, but kiss it is: ambiguous, ambitious and expensive to both parties.

Urbane Mega-Build

Just as mixed in quality are the results of Post-Modern urbanism as interpreted by large developers and civic authorities. The early 1980s saw the widespread acceptance of Jane Jacobs' critique of Modern planning and the great sense of her primary message: mixed uses, mixed ages of building, mixed social groups. Mixture and pluralism – two central tenets of Post-Modernism in all fields – replaced functional zoning and the tabula rasa approach to the city. Most cities in the West adopted a version of Jacobite planning lore, but unfortunately scaled it up to huge size, thus in a sense cancelling one of her chief points: piecemeal growth. The reason for this inversion, as might be expected, was quick profit. In London the Covent Garden district, Broadgate in the City and the massive Canary Wharf area of the Docklands received the Post-Modern formula, often distorted by large size: 'urbane mega-build' was the oxymoronic result.

In America the Rouse Corporation carried out a slightly more yuppified version of the genre, notably in New York, Baltimore and – to my mind the most successful application of the formula – Boston's Faneuil Hall marketplace area. Here they were aided in urban place-making by the considerable experience of Ben Thompson and the infill buildings and towers of Graham Gund and Adrian Smith of SOM. The mixture of functions and new and old structures, the carving out of positive public space, the contextualism and ornament of the architecture are all of a generally high standard. A certain debt in pleasing the crowds is, ironically, owed to Disneyland where corporate street theatre was first formulated, but of course Disney himself learned this Main Street formula, in turn, from successful European cities.

Furthermore, like the mega-developments of Battery Park City in New York and Canary Wharf in London, there was even a positive social policy introduced which supported the visual pluralism. Hiring a minority workforce, reserving a certain percentage of employment for blacks, women and the disadvantaged, and encouraging small businesses have led to a social diversity that is the essence of urbanity. Enlightened planning everywhere in the 80s was based on a similar mixture of public and private co-operation which transcended the either/or categories of socialism or capitalism. A planning authority might lay down the ground rules, supposedly provide most of the infrastructure and then let private developers build and reap the profits. Such a post-modern mixture might be called 'socitalist' to underscore its hybridisation as socialised capitalism, a fusion the Japanese have perfected.[10]

Name it what you will, this synergetic enterprise was responsible for the most successful urbanism. Particularly important was the IBA (International Building Exhibition) in Berlin, a project of town building that continued over a decade, from the late 1970s to the late 1980s. In addition to the aforementioned Post-Modern formulae there was a particular emphasis in Berlin on perimeter block planning – that is, pushing the building right up to the street edge on four sides of a city block to allow maximum shelter for the backyards and the recreation of city street life. As Jane Jacobs pointed out, this life is essential to the functioning of a city, and as Leon Krier added, it provides the basic visual and circulation logic. Also the policy of choosing several architects for a site was emphasised, so that the city might once again have the visual variety and typological diversity that has always been its strength. Broadgate and Canary Wharf in London and Battery Park City in New York followed IBA's example in carrying out these principles, albeit with less sensitivity.

Another significant strategy the authorities adopted, under the guidance of Josef Paul Kleiheus and Robert Krier among others, was to set up a competition system that selected some of the most creative international architects. This resulted, negatively, in a certain number of signature-buildings and, positively, in an equal number of well-designed housing layouts – perhaps as much as 30 per cent of all the schemes over ten years. Two of the best projects were designed by the California-based team of Charles Moore and the Italian-based team of Aldo Rossi, and in both cases the architects were spurred to perform above their average for the natural reason that they were placed on the centre stage of a major city along with their international peers. Moore, Ruble and Yudell's housing was Schinkelesque in front and picturesque on the garden side, whereas Rossi's was industrial classicism on both sides of the perimeter wall. General guide-lines did not mandate a variable Post-Modern Classicism everywhere – and by the end of IBA development the competition system was favouring the Deconstructive approach of Daniel Libeskind – but in general, new versions of a traditional grammar and street layout were preferred.

In many ways IBA represented the high point of Post-Modern urbanism and it has become the model for other cities such as Frankfurt (where a central district has been developed) and Odense in Denmark (where the various types of new housing are even being evaluated by sociologists). This is all very worthy and enlightened. If the projects have an obvious fault, however, it is that housing alone cannot make a city either functional or urbane. Planning authorities in Europe do not appear to have the power or political will to commission a really rich mixture of public, commercial and domestic building. Paris, of course, is the notable exception where its *grands projets* are predictably all civic, public and imperial in scope. No doubt these were realised only for the last reason: because French presidents, in the manner of Louis XIV, have a tradition of leaving behind large objects that mark their reign. Is it a surprise that this memorialising urge has resulted for the most part in Late- rather than Post-Modernism? Could it be that monuments on this scale, without any great social idealism, *have* to be abstract?

Be that as it may, a really balanced urbanism has eluded all countries. In America and Britain, where the political orientation favours market-led solutions, the developer has played a larger role than the planning authority. When the conditions are right, when there is an economic boom and a street-wise entrepreneur, this can lead to whole tracts of a city undergoing immediate urban transformation. The Los Angeles-based Jon Jerde partnership characteristically finds itself simultaneously re-designing 20 or 30 'hearts' of a city that had suffered cardiac arrest in the 60s and 70s as the combined result of Modernist planning and the flight to the suburbs. Jerde regenerates these old centres, again with the Jacobite remedy of mixed uses, mixed ages and mixed types of buildings: but his injection of public space, street theatre and commerce make it work economically. Whenever a central district needs regeneration, such as downtown San Diego, or whenever a 60s sprawl needs tying together, such as the suburban shopping mall, Jerde provides his medicine: shopping arcades, pedestrian space, and lots of street activity *à la* Rouse and Disney. As architecture the results are dayglo Michael Graves; as urbanism they are sensible versions of street planning. The missing factor is, again, the public realm of real civic buildings: commerce, as the single urban generator, is only marginally more effective in creating the city than housing.

The most ambitious urbane mega-build in America is no doubt Battery Park City, a 'city within the city' in downtown New York near Wall Street and next to the World Trade Centre. Here on a 92-acre landfill site on the Hudson River, a state agency teamed up with several developers including the largest in the world, the Canadian group Olympia and York, to produce urbanity at a massive and, it has to be added, lumpish scale. Planned again on Jacobite and Post-Modern principles by Cooper, Eckstut Associates, the scheme consists of two major residential areas north and south of the World Financial Centre (WFC).

This complex of four squat skyscrapers contains seven and a half million square feet (the equivalent of three Empire State Buildings), six million of which will house office workers beavering away for giant corporations (inside are the headquarters of American Express, Merrill Lynch and Dow Jones). Surrounding these 30,000 workers there will be by 1993, 40,000 upper-income residents. The figures, like some of the repetitive architecture, can be fatiguing.

The WFC cost over $1.5 billion while the whole scheme is reckoned to finally cost $4.5 – although these figures were 1986 estimates and may work out higher.[11] Even greater sums are being spent by Olympia and York and others in the London Docklands and, when one thinks of the figures in the context of Disney, Graves, Philip Johnson *et al* the conclusion is reached that the billion dollar development has become as common to Post-Modernists as it was to the Modernists (even if a billion isn't what it used to be). One doesn't have to be a Marxist to believe that *all* this development has enough in common to make its stylistic and philosophical differences marginal. Too big is too big, whatever the approach.

Nevertheless for Paul Goldberger and many astute critics 'Battery Park City is a Triumph of Urban Design', because it mixes public and private values in about equal measure.[12] The public amenities include a riverside esplanade, lots of open space filled with art works commissioned for a specific site, and Rector Park – what Goldberger calls the best of its kind in New York since Gramercy Park. Also it follows the general aesthetic guide-lines concerning massing, cornice lines, masonry materials and tripartition (most buildings have a defined base, middle and top). This creates the unity with variety that is the hallmark of urbanity. As for the private sector and contribution, this includes not only the housing as a function, but the fact that more than 15 developers own the properties – so public and private values do interact synergetically in many ways.

Architecturally the results are impressive but flawed, and like Graves' work for Disney they lead me to reassert the Ivan Illich Law of Diminishing Architecture. Since no one paid the slightest attention when I divulged this hypothesis 15 years ago, and since it now looks true beyond reasonable doubt, I will ask the reader's indulgence for repeating it: 'for any building type there is an upper limit to the number of people who can be served before the quality of an environment falls'. QED 40,000 inhabitants plus 30,000 workers placed in an environment run up in ten years results in, well, wallpaper architecture.

Given these limitations Cesar Pelli has produced very intelligent, sensuous and creative wallpaper. For one thing his towers set back, thin out and change their window/wall ratio as they rise – some up to 50 stories – thus reducing the visual bulk. For another thing the granite at the base decreases in quantum jumps just as the reflective glass increases, thus creating the interesting illusion of a building within a building within a building – or else another new idea, 'the peeling building'. These squat-scrapers also share similar granite bottoms and related copper tops. It's true the distinctive hats – stepped, pyramidal and domed – do not symbolise anything other than 'unity in variety' and are thus only a superior form of wallpaper, but at least they *are* visual culminations.

On the inside of these office labyrinths Pelli has designed extremely elegant domed spaces which transform the wallpaper into flat repetitive patterns which are cut across to accentuate their applied thinness. At these points the Post-Modernism is explicit and masterful: we know that he intends the sign of insubstantiality to be an essential part of the morality and aesthetic because the cuts are so abrupt. The centre of the whole scheme, indeed Battery Park City's 'heart', is the vaulted Winter Garden which now wraps the theme of the exterior skin into a series of telescopic folds. These repeat in section the stepped layering of the towers and thus conceptually bring the whole scheme into focus. But the Winter Garden is again a flawed masterpiece, a battle between economy and gesture with no clear winner. As an interior space it is extremely urbane and pleasant, especially in the cold season when the 16 palm trees and warmth are most welcome. Equally positive are the views to all sides: down the thin end of the telescope towards the World Trade Centre towers, down the other end towards the Hudson River. Only the awkward shapes of the exterior look unfortunate and mean, as if the developer had cut back the money. This of course reminds us of the four towers, which look as if the planners had shortened and fattened them.

If Battery Park City is the best of urbane mega-build, then it shows this genre still has a way to go before it constitutes an entirely balanced fabric. No city hall or church graces this city within the city. There is just the typical over-concentration of offices and housing, the over-specialisation which distorted Modernism and still plagues its offspring. We have become so accustomed to this situation, it is so ubiquitous, that it now escapes comment, and there seems little political will to do anything about it. Thus if we are to continue with 'fast-food mega-build' – a

perforce, deal with the micro-scale of city fabric need more explicitly formal models, and for this the idea of small block design, or village planning, has recently come to the fore. It constitutes one of the ways Post-Modern precepts overlap with, but don't quite match, traditional ones.

Designing a city of small blocks is a goal that has appealed to three entirely different urban theorists – Jane Jacobs, Leon Krier and Christopher Alexander – no doubt for completely different reasons. But the three agree on its suitability because of one point: it allows a piecemeal growth which is economically and aesthetically desirable. Small block planning lets feedback work, whether it concerns an investment, or a visual decision. For this model of the Italian hill town, or 'organic village' as it is also known, is a stereotype appreciated now by everyone, thanks to tourism and the media. The force of the idea gains further weight, not only because of this popular and variegated acceptance – by three different schools of design – but also because of a recent fourth and fifth. Some Deconstructionists, particularly Frank Gehry, have now added their weight to the bandwagon. Prince Charles has climbed aboard and soon, no doubt, President Bush will agree it is a good thing. It is, especially when compared with the superblocks of Le

CESAR PELLI, WORLD FINANCIAL CENTRE, BATTERY PARK CITY, NEW YORK

horrible phrase and an unfortunate reality – then it is progress of a kind when it reflects Jane Jacobs principles and is carried out with the skill of a Pelli. This is of course no substitute for the creation of real urbanity.

Village Planning as Model
The big cities of the world have expanded into huge regional megalopoli relatively recently, mostly in the last 30 years. The growth of the Boston to Washington megalopolis ('Bosh-Wash' as it was called in the late 1960s) is typical and has its counterpart in Europe, Japan, Mexico and the Greater London region. Like all these communicational sprawls, it has too many interlinked causes to analyse here. But one thing can be quickly said. No society is politically or economically equipped to deal with this inflation on the macro-scale, and so imbalances in fabric will continue to occur. Lucky is the city that can just keep its transportation system up to date, never mind its overall plan, or balance in structure.

Chaos theory and self-organising theory derived from the Nobel laureate Ilya Prigogine are being put forward as proper ways to conceive of, and perhaps contain, this runaway growth – for instance the anarchic beauty of Tokyo.[13] But architects who must,

Corbusier, or those of the mega-builders.

Interestingly enough, the village model has been applied where one might least expect it: to the huge office building and multinational bank. The probability was that these leviathans would continue in the Modern corporate mould, building highly visible tributes to their might as they have done since the 1870s, with one freestanding monument trumping the previous one into obscurity: the Woolworth Tower, the Chrysler Building, the AT&T, the Hongkong Bank and, needless to say, the Trump Tower. One doesn't have to be Freud to know what is going on here. But lo, there is now a feminine response to all these upright members – the groundscraper and the undulating body building that hugs the earth, and tries to be green.

In Holland the architect Tom Alberts has broken up the mammoth NMB Bank – with its 2,400 employees – into a cluster of ten brick blobs. These chunky pavilions, as they are also known, snake around the site in an irregular, choppy s-curve thus providing a unique set of profiles from any one place. Gone is the image of the bank as a stiff classical ramrod, or pompous mirrored erection; gone too are the images of bureaucracy and monotony; and back is the image of a medieval village, taller than usual, covered all over with perhaps too many Dutch bricks (3.5 million of them) and full of odd animal and organic metaphors. The architects are dedicated followers of Rudolf Steiner and his anthroposophical method of design, one that stresses ecological sense, passive solar heating and all sorts of humane qualities. While the NMB Bank is not notable as high architecture, it is certainly popular and sensible, especially because it breaks up a large volume and introduces the notion of the street and square into the building (which does, of course, take them from the outside world where they belong).

A few other corporations have attempted a related concept – the Centraal Beheer in Appeldorn and the Colonia Building in Cologne – and we could say the 'office as village' may soon become an accepted model for the future. After all, 60 per cent of the work-force in the First World is destined to work in these post-industrial factories, and each year this population demands more and more amenities to keep on the job. If the corporation does not provide acceptable spaces and services then, as in Los Angeles, the electronic cottage may start to become a more pressing challenge to the central office – at least for a few days each week. In 1990 the London Telecom system estimated that perhaps 20 per cent of the population would soon be telecommuting.

and layered in flat, horizontal planes like the building itself. This correspondence between parts and whole gives both a delightful resonance. Because of one repeated fractal pattern it also makes one see the entire metallic building as a wafting cloud. In the end this office as village is so successful because the architect has adopted a mixed grammar of curves and straight lines and played them at such an intricate scale that he has managed to symbolise the interpenetration of nature and culture. We begin to believe a giant fashion company can work like an organic community: all the functions from design to manufacture and distribution are housed here, and the image of interdependence is so convincing. One wonders if it is a real community?

The most convincing Western example of a corporate village is the recently completed Landeszentralbank in Frankfurt. It nestles so effectively into the urban fabric that many people would overlook its presence altogether. But when they ascend to one of the many surrounding towers – the typical Modern shafts of corporate potency – and look down, they will discover an exception to the tough urban roofscape. There below is not the usual collection of mechanical boxes, but a wild garden of hardy plants – herbs, junipers, polychromatic heather and cacti – all held within a

L TO R: TOM ALBERTS, NMB BANK, HOLLAND; HIROSHI HARA, YAMATO INTERNATIONAL, TOKYO; AJM & BLR LANDESZENTRALBANK, FRANKFURT

In Tokyo the architect Hiroshi Hara has designed an exquisite High-Tech office as village for the international fashion company Yamato. This has a big/smallness that is uncanny, a big volume that is broken up into so many small parts that it looks like a bubbly Italian hill-town of the future: one can't tell quite how large it really is. The room-size forms are layered back and stepped to the right as they rise, as if tiny buildings were clinging to the face of a canyon. The reality is as charming as the photographs suggest, creating, for a change, a corporate world that is pleasantly subdivided and semi-private in parts.

One approaches under a large gate/bridge into a piazza with a flat reflecting pool and polished paving-stones – so highly polished that one can't see the transition between water and masonry. Lighting standards here and elsewhere vary between the abstract and representational. Throughout the stacked village a series of abstracted themes repeat in a transformed way – clouds, shore-lines, geodesic structures, birds and trees – to create a very consistent ornamental programme. These images are not insistent one-liners, as they are in the Disney Kingdom, but much more subtle variations on a set of natural and cultural signs. They are often made of an industrial material – sheet metal, etched glass –

discipline of grey steel tracks, the window cleaning equipment. Here is the typical double-coding of Post-Modernism, and the greening of the industrial landscape.

The Landeszentralbank actually has six hanging gardens as well as the growing roofscape, and all six are in a unique style. Some are modifications of the traditional French garden and set dark green topiary against a flat white pebble background. Others combine the English romantic garden with wandering patterns based on the computer circuit-board. But the point is that each of the six gardens, one floor above ground level, acts as a focus for the cluster of offices which surround it on three sides. These are conceived as houses grouped around a common green court.

Thus the huge corporation, a central bank for others in the region, is broken down into units at a village scale. Instead of these units being stacked vertically as in Norman Foster's Hongkong Bank, or scattered about rather wastefully as in the NMB Bank, they are grouped in an urbanistic pattern that visually welcomes in the rest of the city and reinforces the existing street grid.

The building is convincing not only because of its layout and gardens, but also because of its symbolism and structure. The difference between the underlying steel structure and the visible surface of stone blocks becomes the pretext for the characteristic Post-Modern type of symbolic ornament. Instead of the load-bearing construction of traditionalists, or the curtain wall of Modernists, we find the hung and peeled façade of stone slabs, which are exaggerated in their layering to emphasise their non-structural, but urban role. The intermediate layers of construction are shown because of the peeling process, and the fact that the stone is non-structural is revealed by the cracks between them and their bevelled edges. Thus the ornament derives directly from revealing the truth of construction, as it does in Stirling's work at Stuttgart and elsewhere.

A steel motif in the shape of a T, or tree, or face is repeated in several ways throughout the building, changing its shape to suit the particular context. When the T-shape is on the outside it works as a giant trellis so that growing plants can shield the hanging gardens: here it is surmounted by a delicate, tapering curve appropriately creating the profile of the crown of a tree. On the inside the T-shape is painted in shades of green and the natural imagery is made even more explicit in the piazza where the T-piers are accompanied by potted trees.

If a large corporation is to embody the true urbanity of a village,

of the route, is the grand central piazza: this forms a spine of circulation that connects the six houses of the village. Here would be a true public realm, if only the bank were open to outsiders with one end of this space actually opened to the city. The irony is that the Landeszentralbank has created such a good simulacrum of urban architecture that they should sell it to the authorities to make it actually work. The better the spaces and art and architecture, the more one wants them given over to the public.

Towards a Subtle Urbanism

If a few enlightened corporations are resisting the pressure to create architectural one-liners and instead are concentrating on producing varied urban fabric, then so too are a few museums and art centres. Again this shift towards village planning may not represent much yet in terms of construction, but it does indicate a very real change in paradigm which ought, soon enough, to be followed by building. Three loosely termed cultural centres built in the late 1980s show the way, by James Stirling, Kisho Kurokawa and Antoine Predock. Each is a multi-use art-centre, or part of one, and a convincing piece of urbanism in its own right. Each heralds the development of Post-Modernism towards a more subtle elabo-

 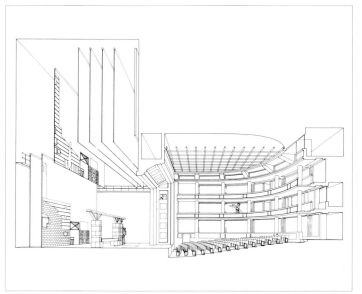

L TO R: AJM & BLR, LANDESZENTRALBANK, 'SIR JOHN SOANE BREAKFAST ROOM' BOARDROOM, LONDON; STIRLING, WILFORD & ASSOCIATES, PAC CORNELL UNIVERSITY

then it must instantly fabricate the variety of spaces and moods that the urban realm creates over time. This the bank does by employing different designers, artists and craftsmen to work on a set of related themes, many of which concern, inevitably, the making and losing of money. By the entrance lobby, where the myth of Dr Faustus is portrayed in murals, and just as one is ascending into the grand, enclosed piazza, are three large golden balls suffering various kinds of distress. The cleanest of these sculptures is the *Deutschmark* as the bank would like it, whereas the other two, with their erosions and protrusions, perhaps represent deflation and inflation. In any case, throughout this five-storey village artworks point up the space or the banking function. The accent on variety extends also into the boardrooms, each of a which is given a different character. For instance the breakfast room from John Soane's house in London, or the Café Aubette of Theo van Doesburg are slightly transformed by the architects into the grammar of layered planes; but still the image is distinctive and recognisable, the mood made *different*. If we must build large chunks of the environment quickly, then it is only right that they incorporate a heterogeneity of taste and represent the pluralism of time.

The most impressive space in the building, and the culmination

ration of symbolism and historical reference than has been seen in the recent past. All three once again make a virtue of small block planning. They may not be great buildings, but they're good ones, and they point Post-Modernism in the right direction.

Stirling and Wilford's Centre for Theatre Arts at Cornell University divides up a very complex mixture of functions into nine chunky blocks and then crashes them together very tightly because of a crowded and precipitous site – teetering on the edge of Cascadilla Gorge. The scheme is in a fragmented classical style for several reasons. One might be its location in a quasi-Mediterranean context: Cascadilla is Spanish for little cascade which is in Ithaca and on a historicising campus where there are many faint memories of the arcadian tradition. A second reason is the architect's previous use of this language, but there is yet another and surprising source for their grammar. It harkens back to Stirling and Gowan's Leicester Engineering Building of 1963, where small volumes were also juxtaposed and elided in a very compact way. They may not have been given the kind of classicising ornament that the architects use today, but their deep structure is the same. It relates to the small grammatical units that can be found in any classical hill town, or urban settlement in the ancient world, a

32

POST-MODERN CONSTRUCTION AND ORNAMENT
CHARLES JENCKS

In the last 15 years ornament has re-emerged as a serious topic of discussion, and the tentative results of this are everywhere to be seen. Decorative elements are applied to buildings for reasons of urban context, functional articulation, compositional harmony and symbolic expression – any of these four reasons being sufficient to justify the extra expense needed to ornament a utilitarian structure. The theoretical and psychological reasons for ornament have been fully clarified by E H Gombrich's *The Sense Of Order*, 1979, almost the last word on compositional logic. Yet for architects committed to building logic, there has to be a fifth rational – construction. How can a valid ornament emerge from the fact of building with steel, concrete, wood masonry and plastic? In the information age, when any material can be shipped anywhere, what is relevant decoration?

The answers that Classicists give today are implausible, if not downright silly: the Ionic and Doric villas constructed today in London pay as little attention to time as to social and constructional realism. On all three counts they are anachronisms. In an unbroken Classical culture where Greek and Latin are still familiar – let us say the 18th century – the Doric order was common enough to be symbolically neutral, to sink below consciousness. And this was much of its point: to be a vernacular about which one didn't have to think. Today, however, it recalls the Dorian tribe, or Ancient Greece or the 18th century world view, or a sentimental attitude to the past – not meanings which are pressing to burst into public life.

Of course anachronisms should be allowed in a democracy – Leon Krier is right about this – and, where one is extending or repairing a traditional urban set-piece, even encouraged. But like Prince Charles' truncated views on the subject, they say very little about valid ornament. In his *Vision of Britain* he asserts only that one can be anachronistic if one wants: 'People say you can't have up-to-date office space, with all its ducts and cables behind a neo-Georgian or more traditional façade. Well, I've looked into this, and you can'. Indeed, only the most extreme technological determinist would deny the fact that you can do with a façade anything that you like; but the significant question is 'what ornamental system is relevant in terms of time, context, culture and construction?'

The system that the Prince was attacking at this point in his film, and book, was Arup Associates' scheme for Paternoster, something he chided as 'watered-down classicism'. However, when one examines the order Arups proposed for the area, its relevance across from St Pauls becomes clear, because it takes up the paired column and rustication themes of the cathedral and then finds contemporary equivalents in terms of constructional realism. Instead of the Corinthian capitals of St Pauls, it proposes a dark void above a thick masonry abacus, a black rectangle which is repeated, at different scale, in the bottom of the arcades and the top attic. The solution was compositionally consistent, structurally relevant and highly appropriate for its context as the supporting background to the cathedral. Had it been built, it would have added to the sequence of Post-Modern ornamental systems that James Stirling, Robert Venturi and Arups themselves have been developing since the mid-70s.

Part of this sequence can be seen at Kingswood and Canons Marsh buildings, both of which create a new tripartite order – of Heroic scale – based on functional realities. They are both highly 'constructed' orders. The former is a bit chunky in its proportions and lack of entasis and transitions, but it sets the stage for further refinements, especially with its interesting background screen which is placed visually halfway up the columns. A square base gives way to a round tubelike shaft, then a flared wooden capital that holds an ultra-thin cornice. Stirling in Berlin and at Cornell has experimented with similar 'tree-columns' although he starts the branching much lower down and exaggerates the contrasts between masonry and steel.

At Canons Marsh, the paired heroic order rests on a high rusticated base, as it would have at Paternoster. Again the capital has an exaggerated flare, but now of only a few (four) branches, This, combined with the light shafts and dark tops, means that the capitals are read as voids, a characteristic Post-Modern device of the 'absent presence'. The quandary in a secular, pluralist age is what to represent here: stylised acanthus leaves and Ionic volutes are clichés which send the wrong message. And yet the eye and the mind demand a culmination at this point. Constructional necessity may solve part of the problem and suggest some of the solution – thin steel 'props' and diagonal braces – but they are still not a representational system.

No doubt as with past orders, necessity is the mother of invention and it must be stylised and turned into a rhetorical sign itself. In both schemes the timber and steel walkway screens, and the window cleaning supports provide the basis for future elaboration. These elements and the branching capitals may, if developed, lead Arup, Stirling and others working on similar solutions, to produce something quite expressive. They may even lead to a canonic PM 'tree Order' – something that shows our continuity with the natural world and its analogy for construction and shade.

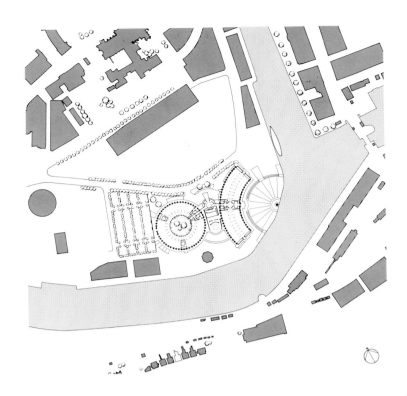

ARUP ASSOCIATES
CANONS MARSH AND KINGSWOOD

The offices for Legal & General at Kingswood, Surrey, and Lloyds bank in Canons Marsh, Bristol, are the most recent in a series of corporate headquarters designed by Arups. Both company's previous buildings had become obsolete, unable to accommodate essential new technology. The sites, however, were outstanding – one urban, one rural.

The Canons Marsh office has a three storey crescent form, contained within stone gable end walls, with a central rotunda and continuous galleria. An intentionally urban scale is reflected in the detailing, proportion of columns and the canopy they support.

The principle architectural benefits of a free standing facade – ease of maintenance and energy saving aside

– is the use of fine components and the best materials. These components are carefully crafted and assembled to bring a distinction and quality to the buildings which reflect their site and setting, rather than the urgency of a construction programme.

The horizontal building at Kingswood is counterbalanced by the central rotunda's brick and stone elements, as well as the corner staircase and service towers that frame the facades. A free standing colonnade and pergola are the primary element of the main façade. Reconstructed columns support a timber lattice work that screens the glazed metal skin behind; enhancing the environmental performance and giving the offices a distinct scale and order.

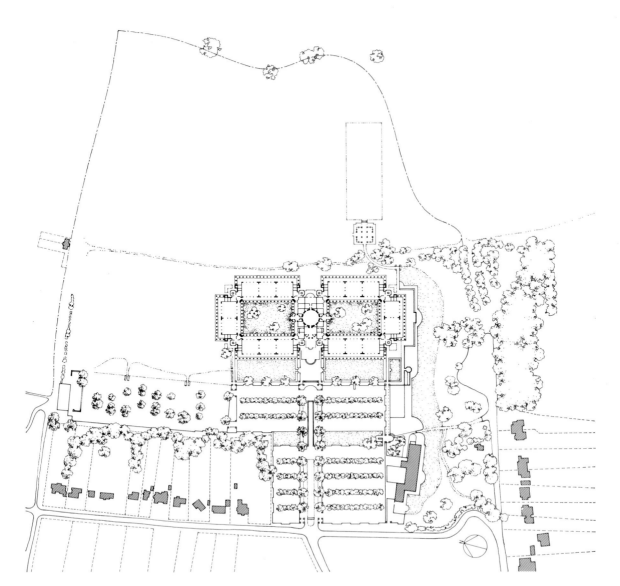

LLOYD'S BANK, CANONS MARSH, BRISTOL: FACADE (*P36*), MODEL (*P38*), SITE PLAN (*P39*, ABOVE), FACADE OVERLOOKING THE HARBOUR (*P39*, BELOW)
OFFICES FOR LEGAL AND GENERAL, KINGSWOOD, SURREY: MODEL (*PP40-41*), FACADE (*P42*), SITE PLAN (*P43*, ABOVE), AERIAL VIEW (*P43*, BELOW)

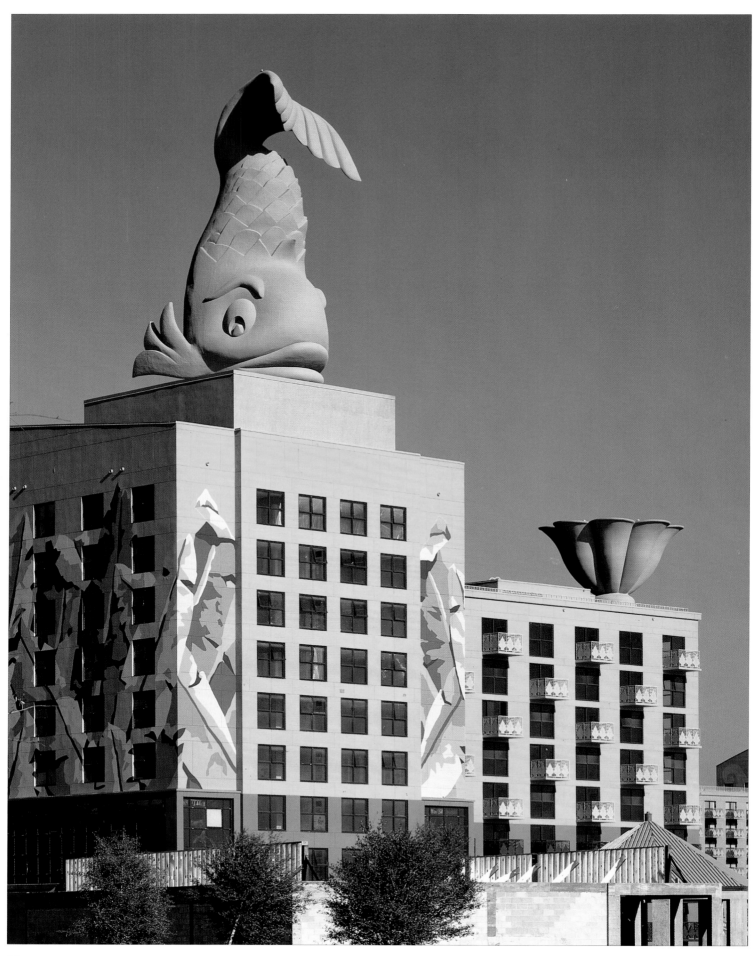

44

MICHAEL GRAVES
WALT DISNEY DOLPHIN AND SWAN HOTELS

The first view of the Dolphin Hotel is the best. We drive in along Disney World's entrance road and come to a bridge and the foliage opens out to the right, and there they are, the Swan and Dolphin, seizing the Florida sky. The Dolphin dominates. Its high gable – the biggest gable in the world? – looms over the Swan's flat curve. In this frontal view the gable is magisterial, the lord of the sky. From the side it is so narrow that it looks rather silly, like the false gables that have been cropping up in shopping centres lately.

The Swan is in every way lesser than the Dolphin and a preparation for it. It has no major spaces of its own. One should pass right through its pinched central corridor to the giant's causeway of massive stones that leads from it across the lagoon to the Dolphin's wholly incredible facade. Painted banana leaves clothe its high, flat walls at Jack-and-the Beanstalk scale and a series of Venus scallop shells directs a heavy cascade of water down from the gable. The shells are flanked by dolphins, the lowest one, the biggest of all, is monumentally supported by free-standing dolphin cut-outs. It is designed with a lip. It slavers. The colour scheme, too, represents an advance for Graves over that of the Swan, which is distinctly lugubrious. Fine colour reproductions of paintings by Matisse are hung every-where, and their shapes and colours are happily echoed throughout the building.

At first the imagery seem excessive, but one rapidly gets used to it, perhaps numbed. Nevertheless the scale, though large, is very gentle. The piers are screened by trellises, threaded with vines; the dolphin fountain splashes. It makes a good place to sit, one of the few wholly successful lobbies of recent years, devoid of Portmanesque paranoia and Trumpish frump.

No, none of it is real. One can't blame Disney or that. The experience is Dionysian, disorienting. When the wonderful birds – ducks, sparrows, cowbirds, and crows – come and beg pieces of hot dog from us they all act like Disney characters. We have gone mad. But that is what Carnival is for. We have got to disorient ourselves once in a while. Life is altogether more real than we can take. How well do the Swan and Dolphin serve this end? They are far away from the Magic Kingdom and are intended to be the iconographic heart of the new Disney World, which is in my opinion somewhat more pretentious, less appealing, much less affecting than the old. They are very expensive, in no way populaire, housing vast conventions of sober-suited executives who to the innocent eye look out of place in Disney World. **Vincent Scully**

DOLPHIN HOTEL: CONSTRUCTION VIEW OF CONVENTION CENTRE (*P44*); SWAN HOTEL: FACADE (*P45*), VIEW FROM DOLPHIN HOTEL TO SWAN HOTEL (*PP46-47*), 'GARDEN GROVE' CAFE (*P48*), LOBBY (*P49*), PREFUNCTION CORRIDOR (*PP50-51*)

THE NEWARK MUSEUM

The master renovation plan for the Newark Museum encompasses new public facilities, as well as the expansion of support space in all four of the Museum's main buildings.

The design challenge of the master renovation plan was to make a unified ensemble out of the disparate buildings. By emphasising a clearly organised connection of the buildings, this design enables visitors to orientate themselves easily to the expanded complex.

Providing a variety of room shapes and sizes throughout the renovation contributes to the visitor's sense of the organisation of the whole. The passages that connect the three major skylit spaces – the South wing's new side entry, the main building's original
central court, and the new three storey atrium in the North wing – provide a sequential hierarchy of movement which allows the visitor to feel orientated within this very large complex. The museum has been painted several shades of white and pale colours that in a subtle way articulate the architecture and yet do not detract from the display of the collection.

The museum's collection is so diverse that a variety of spaces is necessary; the four existing buildings are also so disparate that a hierarchical plan arrangement helps guide the visitor. In order to fulfil the Museum's goal of accessibility to all, an articulate, figurative architectural language provides an inviting and familiar place to visit and explore.

ALL PICTURES IN THIS ARTICLE ARE BY ESTO

ROBERT STERN
DISNEY CASTING CENTRE

Once upon a time there were buildings and there was architecture and the two had very little to do with each other. There was a great kingdom called Disney, and in it were many, many buildings, and while most of them were fun to look at, they were not architecture. And then one day a new prince named Michael came to rule the kingdom, and he decreed that architecture could be just as much fun as buildings. And so the kingdom filled up with hotels named after swans and dolphins, and office buildings with caryatids modeled after the Seven Dwarfs and doorways shaped like Mickey Mouse ears. And everybody lived happily ever after.

If Walt Disney's moviemakers were telling the story of their company's extraordinary building binge, it would probably sound something like the paragraph above. And the Disney version, if we can call it that, would not be so far from the truth. In six years, Disney has transformed itself from a builder of theme parks to one of the most ambitious patrons of serious architecture in the world. Today, it is no exaggeration to talk of the Walt Disney Company in the same breath as Cummins Engine, Johnson Wax or IBM – corporations that have made architecture an essential part of their image.

It's easy to understand what the International Business Machine Corporation has gotten out of its architectural patronage – the sleek designs of its buildings connotes the sense that the company approaches its business with sophistication and self-assurance. But it's harder to grasp what's in it for Disney, a company that has been wildly successful at producing what might be considered the absolute opposite of serious architecture. You go to Disneyland not for aesthetic uplift but to participate in a vast show – to walk through a three-dimensional version of a movie, and to be comforted by Disney versions of the familiar, which are invariably sweeter, gentler, in every way more appealing than the buildings of the real world.

Where does big-time architecture fit into all of this? Is there really room for intellectual and aesthetic challenge in the Disney experience? The real genius of the Disney transformation – and the reason everything Disney is doing is much more significant than it at first appears – lies in the way in which the company cannily figured out that architecture itself was undergoing a vast change in the last decade, a change that could dovetail perfectly with Disney's corporate needs. When IBM started commissioning well-known architects to design its buildings, most serious works of architecture were modernist in style and cool and aloof in tone. By the early 1980s, the pendulum had swung towards a much more sensual kind of architecture – that like the Disney Company itself, was concerned with entertainment and image. This is not to minimise the enormous personal role that Michael Eisner, Disney's chief executive, has had in the whole process, Eisner is a remarkably sophisticated and enthusiastic client whose passion for architecture and personal involvement has driven the Disney architecture blitz from the beginning. All of this said, there is a tremendous range in both style and quality to the output of the Disney architectural crusade. Some of the buildings, like Robert Stern's Yacht and Beach Club Hotels now under construction at Walt Disney World, are essentially similar to the 'themed' buildings that the in-house Disney Imagineers produced. Stern was far less literal in his best Disney design so far, the Casting Centre, in Orlando. One part fantasy castle, one part small office building, this enticing little structure manages to be vivid enough to serve as a magnet for potential employees and yet not so frivolous that it is confused with the theme park itself. Stern deftly navigated that tightrope with a building that is whimsical, not to mention gently ironic, in its use of Disney characters as classical decoration. No company has ever tried to market serious architecture to the masses the way Disney is now doing. That is why, whatever the buildings turn out to be like, there can be no doubt that Disney is a force to be reckoned with in the last decade of the 20th century. It is in Disney that the worlds of architecture and entertainment, which have been moving closer to each other for years, have achieved their most powerful intersection yet – becoming so intertwined that it is sometimes impossible to tell any longer which is which. It is a convergence that already means a lot for Disney, and it may turn out in the end to mean even more for architecture   **Paul Goldberger**

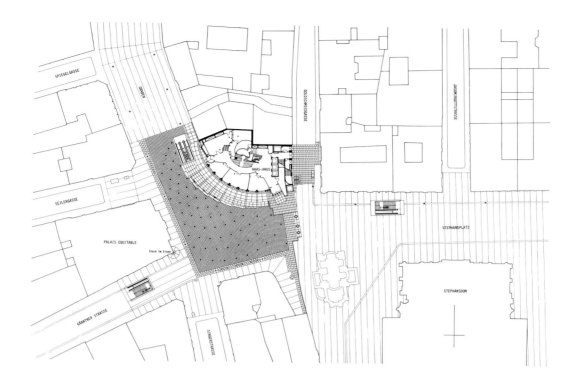

HANS HOLLEIN
THE NEW HAAS HAUS

The Haas Haus is located on the sensitive and historic site facing St. Stephen's Cathederal, and partly recreates the urban structure which was destroyed in the last century. The rounded building line retraces that of the fortification walls of the Roman castrum Vindobona, and the projecting cantilever re-establishes the separation and succession of the ancient city squares.

A living city is continually changing its appearance. Subways, pedestrian zones and a developing urban culture have posed new problems for Vienna's downtown area. The great interest in restructuring the urban picture and in the architectural form of this prominent,

sensitive square finally led to the commisioning of Professor Hans Hollein.

The view of the vicinity of Saint Stephen's Cathedral is an essential element of the design. At the centre of the building, an indoor atrium extends upwards for five floors crowned by a sky-light dome. High-class shops are arranged along gallery-type shopping passages. The floor levels, the escalators and the stairs are organised in such a way that the visitor has a diversified sensation of space and a complete overview of the shops and cafes. A roof-top restaurant affords a splendid view of the City of Vienna.

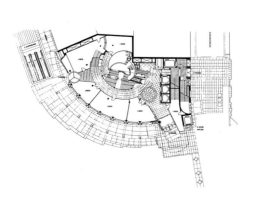

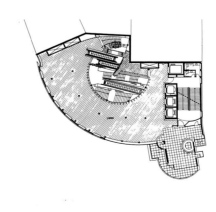

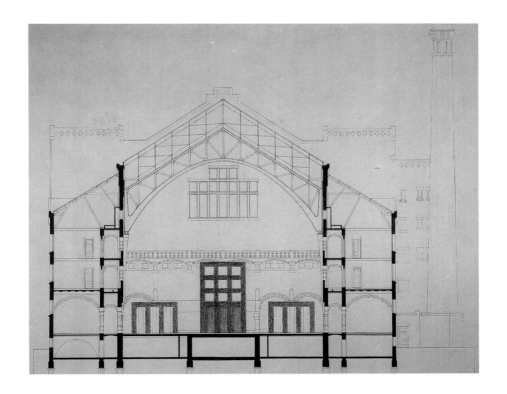

CHARLES VANDENHOVE.
TEMPORARY EXHIBITION IN THE AMSTERDAM BOURSE, 1986.

The exhibition was set up in the great hall of the Amsterdam Stock Exchange, a solid late 19th century monument by Berlage. Vandenhove was determined not to be intimidated by the scale and austerity of the Bourse, or by its reputation as one of the first cathedrals of modernity. Wanting to impose his own personality on the building, he decided to create a colourful and vigorous statement that would mark a violent rupture with the past. At the far end of the hall he erected a cage-like structure in red and vermillion, which seemed to glow like some great machine or temple. Beneath this platform was a small room containing Vandenhove's model of the Salon Royal, later built at the Theatre de Monnai in Brussels. In the centre of the room were two marble obelisks; one capped with an upturned bowl shape, the other with a bronze pyramid. White metallic cables criss-crossed the ceiling above, creating a clear, virtual geometry.* **François Chaslin.**

KISHO KUROKAWA
MUNICIPAL MUSEUM OF MODERN ART, HIROSHIMA

This museum is the first public gallery in Japan to declare itself 'contemporary.' In Hiroshima, contemporary means post-atomic bomb. For a city which has eradicated its pre-war history, the term 'contemporary' has a particular depth of meaning, forging a link between art and peace in a way which might be more difficult for any other city to establish.

The site, at the top of a 50 metre hill, is surrounded by the greenery of a nearby primeval forest and completely shut off from the noise of the city. The area is known as the Hijiyama Art Park and is also home to an outdoor school and a sculpture park. The museum itself is large by Japanese standards, encompassing some 100,000 square feet. In consideration of the view from the city, 60 per cent of the project has been sunk below ground and the visible part of the project - which is nearly 700 feet long - is, in effect, the roof of the gallery.

The design of the roof and wall of the building was inspired by the traditional 'kura' warehouses of the 19th century. As for the façade; stones, tiles, and aluminium are used together to create a synthesis of traditional and modern elements.

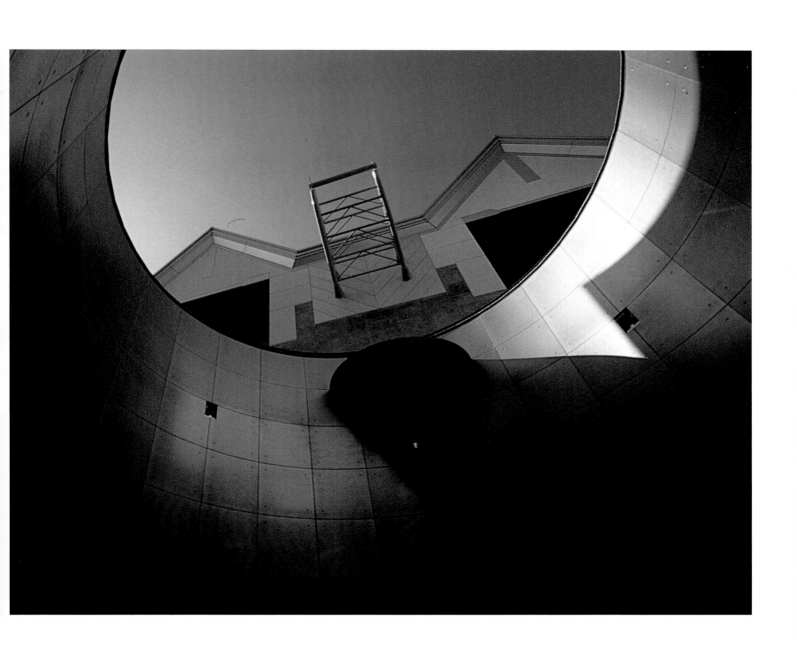

IL GRAN
CANTIE
DI
FUKUOK
PIR
M'87

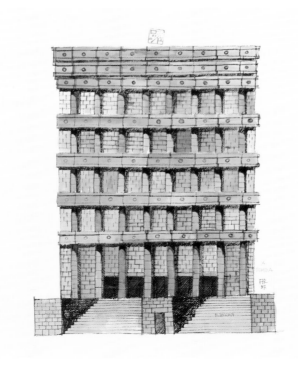

IL PALAZZO

Aldo Rossi, Shigeru Uchida, Ikuyo Mitsuhashi, Ettore Sottssas, Gaetano Pesce, Alfredo Arribas, Shiro Kuramata

The most important aspect of this complex is its position. By connecting the commercial city to an area of recreation and amusement, the new building signals the beginning of the redevelopment of this part of the city. As the single most important property, the Hotel's design could rapidly change the area.

The new building, following the zoning requirements, steps back from the property line allowing the construction of a single storey base level above which the seven storey hotel is situated. The main entrance to the hotel is from the piazza which, like those in many Italian cities, is part of the architecture of the building. From the Piazza it is possible to appreciate the façade of the building and the river landscape.

The façade stone changes colour with different light and weather conditions. When wet – brilliant red. In twilight – gold. The lintels, painted green, cut the plan and give power to the composition. The riverside façade, devoid of windows, acts as a monument – a reference point for the citizens and visitors to Fukuoka. The absence of windows is the result of a conscious effort to accentuate the architectural quality of the façade as pure monument.

Our principal, in this project, is that we build the shell and structure for the architecture of the interiors. We made suggestions to the interior designers who give personality and feeling to the different spaces. The union of different cultures produces dynamic work.

The image of the high, red, gold building standing as a city gate will herald the renaissance of the architecture of the whole city!

Aldo Rossi, Morris Adjmi

INTRODUCING FUKUOKA

In Fukuoka, as one strolls along the lamp lit embankments lining the canals, one sees a panorama of games. These involve fire, fish and various animals that can be seen nowhere else in the world. Many such games and entertainments have oriental subtleties, the significance of which are now lost.

Fukuoka, like any other town in Japan, has many stalls and sales-carts lined up along its waterways. These stalls are quite different to anything in Europe. Often mobile, and dealing in a variety of trades, they have the appearance of small houses. Each one is a kind of restaurant producing its own speciality. As far as I can remember, Italy has many of these small stalls along its main roads, called granita. They cater for cyclists and the occasional truck driver, selling crushed ice drinks prepared with a suspicious looking coloured syrup (I say suspicious because it has exactly the same colours and flavouring as the drinks it is trying to emulate: dark, thick tamarind, sour lemon yellow, peppermint green, and grenadine red). Although this colouring contrasts sharply with the dust-covered bod-

ies of the cyclists, it nicely reflects the bright yellows and blues of their shirts.

How is this related to Fukuoka's Palazzo? The casual reader is likely to overlook the subtle relationship between the artist and his surrounding environment; just as there is a similar tendency to disregard the subtle relationship between the artist's techniques in his work and the immediate physical world. Something like Il Palazzo can't be built upon nothing. Its beauty stems in part from the everyday life that surrounds it; and how the poet to express this passion.

Thinking about it, as in the folk-tales of long ago, the granita strangely beckon us, as if there's a wondrous drug inside. Resembling the rocks in the park that hide a diseased nature – no longer needed – Fukuoka's Palazzo has green veins etched into it by acid making one think of minerals and trees. These are reminiscent of minerals and trees in nature. The green veins are the entrance into the Orient, through to the red stoned mosaics of imperial Persia, the mother of the Occident.
Aldo Rossi

ALDO ROSSI: CONCEPTUAL SKETCHES (*PP80-82*); VIEW OF IL PALAZZO (*P83*); FACADE OVERLOOKING THE RIVER (*P84*); FACADE DETAIL (*P85*); CLOCK TOWER (*P86*); CLOCK TOWER, INTERIOR (*P87, L*); PATH OF THE SUN (*P87, R*)

SHIGERU UCHIDA, IKUYO MITSUHASHI & STUDIO 80: RISTORANTE IL PALAZZO (*PP88-89*); LOBBY (*P90, P91*)

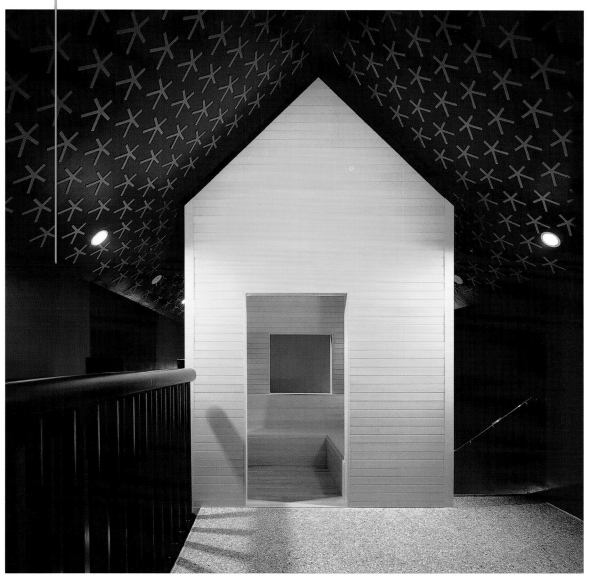

ETTORE SOTTSASS: BAR 'ZIBIBBO' (*P92, P93*); GAETANO PESCE: BAR 'EL LISTON' (*P94*); ALFREDO ARRIBAS: CULTURE RESORT 'THE BARNA CROSSING' (*P95*);
SHIRO KURAMATA: BAR (*P96*)